The Successful Principal

The Successful Principal

Concrete Strategies and Essential Advice

Robert Cunard

ROWMAN & LITTLEFIELD
Lanham • Boulder • New York • London

Published by Rowman & Littlefield
A wholly owned subsidiary of The Rowman & Littlefield Publishing Group, Inc.
4501 Forbes Boulevard, Suite 200, Lanham, Maryland 20706
www.rowman.com

Unit A, Whitacre Mews, 26-34 Stannary Street, London SE11 4AB

Copyright © 2017 by Robert Cunard

All rights reserved. No part of this book may be reproduced in any form or by any electronic or mechanical means, including information storage and retrieval systems, without written permission from the publisher, except by a reviewer who may quote passages in a review.

British Library Cataloguing in Publication Information Available

Library of Congress Cataloging-in-Publication Data Available

ISBN 978-1-4758-3776-6 (cloth : alk. paper)
ISBN 978-1-4758-3777-3 (pbk. : alk. paper)
ISBN 978-1-4758-3778-0 (electronic)

Printed in the United States of America

Contents

Acknowledgments		vii
Introduction		1
1	The Essential Principal	3
2	The Selected Principal	11
3	The New Principal	33
4	The Prioritized Principal	47
5	The Strategic Principal	65
6	The Defined Principal	81
7	The Empowering Principal	97
8	The Motivating Principal	113
9	The Principal in Flow	125
10	The Departing Principal	141
References		151
About the Author		153

Acknowledgments

I am grateful for the support of Kristen Cunard, who accepted and encouraged my choice to become a teacher, just as she accepted and encouraged me, with loving faith, that things would somehow work out. My daughters Candace and Corinne, both of whom became better English teachers and much better writers than me, are inspirations themselves who consistently encouraged me to write my own book one day.

I am grateful for the support of Paul Jessup, the wise and courageous superintendent who took a chance on an out-of-town assistant principal who was nearing his expiration date and made me the principal of La Sierra High School. I am grateful for and proud of the wonderful assistant principals with whom I worked during my ten years as a principal. Will Mynster, Mai Hyunh, Dustin Saxton, Mike Simonson, Jennifer Radeka Schriver, Stuart Caldwell, Eva Valencia, Paula Case, Haig Diribe, and Denise Alvarado were great teammates and friends. These men and women have all gone on to do great things as educational leaders, and they have impacted the lives of thousands.

Lastly, I am grateful to my parents, who raised my brothers and me in such a way that we became readers, writers, talkers, and thinkers, unafraid to take some risks and to see where the next adventure might lead.

Introduction

This book is about how to succeed and thrive as a school principal. You would think that books about how to do this abound, but my search for practical advice led me to very few works. During the ten years I served as a principal, I read what wisdom I could find about being a successful principal, but very little of my reading seemed to adequately capture the dynamics of the principal's unique challenges here and now in 2017. In what other CEO position is the CEO gifted with merely a bully pulpit and an opportunity to build support? A CEO in the business world can hire, fire, set direction, and simply replace those who prefer a different direction; the school principal in most settings has none of those tools available.

One thing that surprises many is that principals report to a group of politicians—school board members—who hire them, fire them, and are often elected by the teachers who the principal is supposed to be leading. The principal who loses one or two votes from the board is cast out—and often with no prospects to ever again lead a school. When people wonder why principals can be just a little boring, they need to recognize the principal's structural conundrum: his title and the public's perception suggests that he has enormous power, but the principal quickly understands just how little power he has. What I learned was that everything you achieve as a principal requires the consent of others. Everything.

This book is my effort to distill the lessons I learned over a successful career in order to help others thrive in their work. Where appropriate, I report what researchers and theorists have to say about various strategies and activities. The book is supported by a website (www.thesuccessful principal.org) that contains an archive of my staff letters, links to some good reading, and materials I developed during my entry planning. You may also reach me directly via the website if you wish. I hope the book proves interesting and useful in your work and that you can take a few things away from it that will help you thrive. Being the principal is demanding, but if you do it well, you can change the world, which is exactly what I hope you do.

ONE

The Essential Principal

A leader is best when people barely know he exists, when his work is done, his aim fulfilled, they will say: we did it ourselves.—Lao Tzu

Stanford University professor Michael Copland best described the challenge of being a principal when he suggested these qualifications for the position:

> Wisdom of a sage, vision of a CEO, intellect of a scholar, leadership of a point guard, compassion of a counselor, moral strength of a nun, courage of a firefighter, craft knowledge of a surgeon, political savvy of a senator, toughness of a soldier, listening skills of a blind man, humility of a saint, collaborative skills of an entrepreneur, certitude of a civil rights activist, charisma of a stage performer, and patience of Job. Salary lower than you might expect. Credential required. (Copland, 2001)

Where do you find *one* soul with these qualifications? More practically, where does the state of California find over 11,500 such individuals to lead their public schools and another 3,000 heroes and heroines to lead the state's private schools? And once these principals are recruited, selected, employed, and paid, the demands of the principalship and the pressures to improve academic achievement, college and career readiness, employability of graduates, the character of those graduates, and the fortunes of a school's athletic teams conspire, not surprisingly, to push principals out of their jobs at a fairly alarming rate. Edward Fuller sums up principal turnover well in the state of Texas:

> Strikingly, only about one-half of newly hired middle school principals remained at the same school for three years, while only 30 percent remained at the high school level for three years. After five years, less than one-half of newly hired middle school principals remained, and only 27 percent of high school principals. . . . Overall, the average tenure for a high school principal in Texas is just over three years—the average high school principal will not see her/his first freshman class graduate. (Fuller, 2012)

Even exceptionally trained principals are at high risk of losing their positions quickly in urban settings. The RAND Corporation conducted a fascinating study that compared 94 first-year principals trained by New Leaders, arguably the highest quality principal training ground in our country, to several hundred other new principals not trained by New Leaders. Burkhauser, Gates, Hamilton, and Schuyler Ikemoto reached several important conclusions:

1. Over one-fifth of New Leaders principals left their positions within two years;
2. Schools that lost a principal saw student performance decline in the subsequent year;
3. Teacher capacity and cohesiveness proved to be the factors most strongly related to improved student achievement (Burkhauser, Gates, Hamilton, and Schuyler Ikemoto, 2012).

The New Leaders program, about which we'll hear more in a subsequent chapter, is a highly developed training program for principals with a nationwide footprint. They created and validated a Transformational Leadership Framework, which they have been teaching to principals across the country for several years. And yet, over 20 percent of their first year principals failed to start a third year as principal at the schools they had been brought in to improve. That should give prospective principals reason to pause before they take that leap of faith.

THE PRINCIPAL IS ESSENTIAL TO SCHOOL IMPROVEMENT

The story of what was achieved at La Sierra illustrates an important point: the principal is essential to school improvement. You don't have to be particularly brilliant, and you will undoubtedly make mistakes as a principal, but school improvement is absolutely possible if you can help dozens of teachers come together to do better work. Todd Whitaker put it best in describing a principal's two choices for improving a school when he wrote:

> There are really two ways to improve a school significantly:
> 1. Get better teachers.
> 2. Improve the teachers you have. (Whitaker, 2003, p. 7)

In most schools, it makes sense to give teachers the only thing the principal really has available to give: some autonomy. Once your best teachers

IN MY EXPERIENCE
The Enormity of the Principal's Challenge

Being a school principal can be exhausting. For the ten years I served as a high school principal, my day at school began at 6:45 a.m. If the day included no evening supervision or other duties, I left school at about 5:00 p.m. A school day can become a whirlwind since the principal is responsible for everything. Everything.

The first high school I led was La Sierra High School, located in Riverside, California; it was very large, enrolling 3,200 students and staffed by over 200 employees. Each of those employees had direct access to me. The traditions of our education system make the school principal responsible for everything, even though others may be hired to look after certain functions, such as athletics, food service, campus cleanliness, safety and security, and community relations.

I tried to spend at least half of each school day in classrooms observing instruction and learning alongside our students and staff. Those walk-throughs included dozens of conversations with students and teachers each day. At La Sierra, we had a morning nutrition break, which I, my four assistant principals, one police officer, and 12 campus supervisors monitored. Then it was back to class for everyone until the first of our two lunches occurred.

Again, I had to supervise both lunches while eating my own lunch in the 15 minutes between the two student lunch periods. Following the lunches, I had my daily meeting with my administrative assistant, where we managed my inbox and my meeting calendar. If I had office work, the early afternoon was when it usually got done. Afternoons were taken up with meetings and athletic supervision. Most weeks, I stayed at school into the evening three times, attending and supervising athletics, arts events, and additional functions related to just being the principal. On an average day, I walked about five miles just doing my job.

But the foregoing describes an average day, a good day. When you are the mayor of a small city, as my superintendent told me I effectively was, you know there's a crisis coming; you just don't know when.

One day during the nutrition break in the fall of my first year at La Sierra, 50 students faced off against each other to fight: African Americans versus Latinos. Defusing that crisis and establishing a new tone at La Sierra consumed me for the rest of that first year. There were other crises in subsequent years. A head football coach quit one week before the season was to begin when I would not fire the athletic director. A much-loved senior student became ill and died in spite of the very best medical care available. These crises would inevitably detract from my focus on my primary mission at La Sierra: improving student academic achievement and keeping the school from being sanctioned by our state and labeled a failing school. Sometimes being the principal felt a lot like just trying to keep my head above water as wave after wave washed in and held me underwater yet again.

But I persisted, and as I came to understand La Sierra's gifts, I also began to know its teacher-leaders, and that is where the real gold in the school would

(continued)

eventually be mined. The school had tried a number of different things to improve learning, but those initiatives had been determined by people other than the school staff, and they had achieved only limited success. It was easy to see why district-driven initiatives had not been implemented across all classrooms at La Sierra:

1. There were over 130 teachers, and monitoring their compliance was basically impossible with just five administrators, most of whom were tied up dealing with student misconduct most of the day;
2. The teachers' union was particularly powerful at the school and in the district, which made it easy for teachers to resist new things;
3. For the four years prior to my becoming the principal, the school had literally hired 25 new teachers each year, most from job fairs in the Midwest. Many of these teacher imports stayed at La Sierra for just a few years before either moving back home or getting jobs in more affluent districts closer to the ocean.

No wonder it was difficult to successfully implement a school-wide program or strategy.

It became clear to me that the best path forward for La Sierra would be to unleash the creative power of the staff through collaboration rather than implementing another centrally driven initiative. A few department leaders joined me in learning about the Professional Learning Community (PLC) model from Richard and Becky DuFour. We began a slow, deliberate movement toward distributed leadership by the various academic departments.

I started canceling faculty meetings and turning them over to departments. Some department meetings weren't very productive at first, but teacher-leaders began to emerge and get energized, and I started to see new instructional practices, happier teachers, and better results. In my third year, student achievement just took off. We exceeded my own stretch goal for state testing. We saw huge increases in the number of students who were college eligible. Student misconduct went way down because students were experiencing more academic success. We stopped needing to hire 25 teachers a year because teachers chose to stay at La Sierra.

In my fourth year, La Sierra was in its heyday. Happy, energized teachers developed innovative lessons and systems to ensure that students were learning. Other schools began to visit us to learn about some of those innovations. College eligibility moved from every fifth student to every third student. Instead of being a troubled school where kids fought each other in groups, we had become a school where kids were proficient in their academic subjects, attended school at an astonishing rate, and treated one another with kindness. We were able to achieve dramatic improvements at La Sierra by simply coming together and doing better work, and the school continued to improve students' academic achievement after my departure because its instructional improvements had been implemented by teachers who had designed them, who took ownership of student learning, and who did not stop doing that work after my departure.

realize that you will support their creativity in the PLC process, your school will become a more interesting and effective place.

So how can the principal be essential in the process of a school's improvement? After all, he will likely do little on his own that will improve what happens in the classrooms. However, the principal can teach teacher-leaders and the faculty how to better collaborate. He can specify some big-picture goals each year, and ask that the teachers' collaborative work somehow support attainment of those goals. Doesn't sound like much, does it?

And yet, this is a strategy that improves a school. As the principal becomes trusted and releases responsibility for student learning to the staff, they will willingly take ownership of pacing plans, best instructional practices, assessments, the data that emerge from those assessments, and systems for reteaching when those assessments show that students hadn't yet learned something well enough.

Contemporary research supports the idea that the work of the principal can have a profound impact on student learning. Researchers consistently report that where they find great schools, they find effective principals. They never seem to find great schools led by poor principals, though it's clear that there are plenty of unsuccessful principals out there. Just look at the turnover rate. There is a raft of craft knowledge and research supporting the essential role of the principal in school improvement.

As far back as 1983 in his landmark report on American high schools, Ernest Boyer reported, "In schools where achievement was high and where there was a clear sense of community, we found, invariably, that the principal made the difference" (Boyer, 1983, p. 219). Roland Barth, founder of the Harvard Principals Center, described the importance of the principal in the following four points:

- The principal is the key to a good school. The quality of the educational program depends on the school principal.
- The principal is the most important reason why teachers grow—or are stifled on the job.
- The principal is the most potent factor in determining school climate.
- Show me a good school, and I'll show you a good principal (Barth, 1990, p. 64).

Boyer and Barth based their statements on ethnography—the case studies of individual schools. In time, researchers did more work and conducted more studies, trying to get at the impact of the principal on the school. One of the seminal documents in this movement was produced by Leithwood, Seashore Louis, Anderson, and Wahlstrom in 2004 with the support of the Wallace Foundation.

The Wallace Foundation has invested significant funding in school improvement and has taken a particular interest in the role of the principal. Their key finding was remarkably clear:

> Leadership is second only to classroom instruction among all school-related factors that contribute to what students learn at school. (Leithwood, Seashore Louis, Anderson, and Wahlstrom, 2004, p. 3)

It also turns out that the principal's leadership is even more essential in challenging schools, as their report went on to note that

> demonstrated effects of successful leadership are considerably greater in schools that are in more difficult circumstances. Indeed, there are virtually no documented instances of troubled schools being turned around without intervention by a powerful leader. (Leithwood et al., 2004, p. 5)

More recently, Michael Fullan has contributed a great deal to the research about the efficacy of the principal through his work with large systems in Canada and the United States. He argues that the principal's influence may be even greater than first described:

> [T]here is clearly a multiplier effect if the principal helps, directly and indirectly, 30 or more teachers become dramatically more effective in their teaching. (Fullan, 2010, p. 14)

SOMEONE HAS TO CONDUCT THE ORCHESTRA

Many have wondered why schools even need principals. Indeed, the very title of *principal* is a truncated version of the original position title from England, which was *principal teacher*. When schools were very small, featuring just a few classrooms, this designation made sense. But most schools are much larger now, particularly secondary schools, and their managerial and leadership needs are big and complex. Whereas a small school might be thought of in musical terms as akin to a barbershop quartet, the big schools we see today across our country are really much more like orchestras, and someone simply has to conduct the orchestra if it is to make beautiful music. As the principal becomes a more confident conductor, the musicians (faculty) will become better players and will make better music together than they had before.

This book is about how to succeed and thrive as one of those conductors in a school: how to be a successful principal. You would think that books about how to do this abound, but there seem to be very few. This is surprising since, as we have seen, the principal is such an essential component of a successful school. If you believe teachers are artists, then getting them to work together in ways that complement one another and that magnify their skills and grow their talents is the principal's chief concern. And while that work may not, at first, seem terribly difficult, thousands of people will tell you differently. Talented, driven teachers regularly tell their principals, "I can't imagine doing your job."

We need to find and develop men and women who not only can do the job of school principal, but who can thrive in that job and grow the skills of others. The success of our schools and our society requires that our schools be well led. There are many who wish to serve as principals (principal recruitments in Southern California routinely feature over 100 applicants), but it's clear that we have not done a good enough job of sharing our knowledge about what works.

The chapters that follow will reveal some key strategies any principal can employ to improve their school. But before a principal can get to work improving a school, he or she needs to be appointed to serve in that position, which is itself a huge challenge addressed in our next chapter.

CHAPTER 1 KEY POINTS AND STRATEGIES

1. There is high turnover in the principal's office. The average high school principal will not see his or her first freshman class graduate.
2. Being the principal is physically and emotionally demanding. Every employee and an entire community expect to have direct access to the principal.
3. The principal does not have to be a charismatic leader in order to be successful.
4. There is a solid research consensus that the principal can improve student achievement across an entire school.
5. The successful principal finds a way to conduct the faculty orchestra so that it makes beautiful music.

Two

The Selected Principal

Do not hire a man who does your work for money, but him who does it for the love of it. —Henry David Thoreau

While being a successful principal is difficult, being selected to serve as a principal can be an even more daunting challenge. The selection process is notoriously subjective, and it can be fraught with politics. In some communities, the selection of a new principal can even become a compromise between the teachers' union, the board of trustees, interests in the community, and the superintendent. Sometimes, a principalship is filled without any selection process, as district leaders simply transfer existing administrators to fill openings. But still, someone gets that position, and there are things one can do to increase the likelihood of being selected to lead a school.

We have many schools, and they all need principals. The most recent data reported by the National Center for Education Statistics shows us that there are 115,540 public and private principals in the United States. The average salary of public school principals in the 2011–2012 school year was $90,500, while the average salary of private school principals was much less, checking in at $65,300.

The overwhelming majority (80 percent) of public school principals are white, while 87 percent of private school principals were white. Just over half of all principals are female (though just 30 percent of high school principals are women), and the average age of all principals is 48 (Bitterman, Goldring, and Gray, 2013, p. 3). The United States Department of Labor (2016) expects the occupational category of elementary and secondary school administrators to grow nationally during the ten year period of 2014–2024 by a factor of 6 percent, or 14,000 jobs.

Additionally, we have already seen that there is fairly strong turnover in principals' offices, particularly in challenging urban communities. There are principal jobs out there. So how does one go about getting one? The ten lessons that follow are a good place for an aspiring principal to start.

LESSON 1: TAKE NO SHORTCUTS— EARN THE MA

While there are a variety of pathways toward a career in school leadership now, the best pathway remains the traditional one: taking the extra time and earning the MA instead of merely taking a test, as is possible now in many states. Earning the advanced degree brings with it several advantages. Aspiring principals will meet and learn alongside classmates from a variety of school districts and school settings, and they will benefit from them in ways they may not fully understand while immersed in the degree program. Pursuit of the graduate degree in school administration often helps the aspiring administrator to grow her network of colleagues, mentors, and friends. And pursuing the graduate degree is challenging; candidates will have to push themselves to work hard in many courses, just as they will be pushed once they become administrators.

LESSON 2: PUT YOURSELF OUT THERE

The second benefit of pursuing the MA is that various assignments and the fieldwork requirement will require aspiring administrators to seek out experienced administrators at work in order to learn from them, to complete specific assignments, and to do those assignments well. There is always a lot of work to be done in any school setting, and an aspiring administrator enrolled in a graduate program will find, if she seeks them out, that there are many opportunities to contribute and to learn while pursuing her degree. Doing those additional assignments well is an important part of growing one's reputation.

Aspiring principals often begin their pursuit of an administrative license and a graduate degree while being incredibly busy. Teaching itself can be an all-consuming career, and many who pursue positions in school leadership do so while raising a family and struggling to make ends meet. On top of teaching, graduate school, and the demands of home life, aspiring principals are often confronted with opportunities to do more and to learn more. Aspiring administrators become teacher-leaders, perhaps chairing their grade level or academic department.

In secondary schools, aspiring administrators are confronted with many opportunities for personal and professional growth. They often sponsor school clubs. They may coach athletic teams. They may serve on curriculum revision teams, or they may serve as technology leaders. Over the course of a teaching career, many opportunities to learn will present themselves, and successful administrators learn that investing in oneself is always wise.

LESSON 3: BECOME AN EXCELLENT TEACHER AND CO-ADMINISTRATOR

One of the great truths about hiring people is that their performance in previous positions is an excellent indicator of how they are likely to perform in a new position. This essential element is baked into the process for hiring school administrators—especially when you come to realize that each of the traditional positions in the principal pathway (teacher, assistant principal, principal) is a much different job than the one before it.

What a teacher does is much different from what an assistant principal does, and it surprises many when they discover that a principal's work is much different than an assistant principal's work—but it is. Since each of these promotional positions is so different than the one before it, how do hiring committees make their decisions? Simply put, hiring committees look for excellence in past positions, not adequacy, excellence. Excellence means going above and beyond the norm in terms of work ethic and, ultimately, results.

The very first requirement to move from the classroom to the assistant principal's office is excellence as a teacher. A prospective principal must also look for things to do while teaching that will help her stand out and build a reputation. Here are a few things the aspiring administrator may wish to consider doing during her teaching in order to stand out:

- serve as a grade-level or department leader;
- serve as a Professional Learning Community (PLC) team leader;
- teach an International Baccalaureate or Advanced Placement course;
- teach in a special program (AVID, Project Lead the Way, a CTE concentration);
- serve as a testing coordinator;
- lead a site committee during accreditation or compliance review;
- serve on or lead the school's Technology team;
- serve on the Site Council;
- serve as the teacher representative to the PTA;
- serve as a union representative;
- advise a school club or class; or
- serve as a coach in the school's athletic program.

It sometimes surprises people that service to the teachers' union is desirable, but one learns a great deal from that experience, which proves invaluable later in a career in an administrative role. Many believe in the value of coaching in a school's athletic program because it has a way of opening one's eyes to the bigger picture in kids' and a community's lives.

Coaches learn so much from the experience, which can make them much better principals later in life. Each of the aforementioned positions also provides the potential administrator with something essential: another venue in which to learn.

LESSON 4: NO NEED TO RUSH

While there are men and women who do become principals while in their 30s, experience reveals that most people need more time to learn because being an educational leader simply requires more wisdom and experience than might seem obvious at first. The principal needs a foundation of teaching knowledge strong enough and broad enough to be able to support the needs of diverse teachers in a school.

She needs a variety of cultural experiences in order to be culturally competent with all aspects of a community. She needs to know enough about testing, data reporting, and analysis in order to bring the right level of expertise and authority to a district and community so that they will trust what she says when she is their principal. She needs to understand teachers, the culture of their profession, and the norms of her community in order to properly administer student discipline.

Beyond all these things, though, the successful principal needs to have developed some of the wisdom that comes with experience. This wisdom and perspective becomes critical when dealing with families in challenging situations. It makes a big difference when a new principal has a wide variety of teaching, leadership, and coaching experience. Serving as a teacher-leader better prepares her to serve as a mentor and coach to teachers. If she has served as a coach, it will make it easier for her to make wise decisions in matters related to athletics—which can be highly emotional and time-consuming in the high school setting. It also matters if an administrator is a parent, because it can help her better understand what parents are feeling when they are in her office dealing with a difficult situation. It can make her a better administrator—and it can also make her a better parent.

The last thing an aspiring school administrator still teaching should know is this: keep teaching until you feel like you've gotten everything you can out of your teaching experience. Once you leave the classroom and become an administrator, you're probably not going back to the classroom—unless something difficult happens in your administrative career.

You'll never be closer to the kids than you are as a teacher. You'll never be surer of your direct impact on kids than you are as a teacher. And you'll never have a better schedule than you do as a teacher. If you're happy and fulfilled as a teacher, keep doing it until you just know you have to step out and move into the administrative realm.

LESSON 5: YOU MAY HAVE TO MOVE

One of the challenges of moving from the classroom to the administrative office is that one nearly always has to change schools, and many candidates find that they have to change districts in order to move from teaching to administration. This is difficult for many in K–12 education because most aspects of the profession are designed to prevent people from moving.

In California, teachers are granted permanent status (what the press calls tenure) at the beginning of the third consecutive year of regular teaching service. During the first two years, as most everyone knows, teachers in California are considered probationary and can simply be told in the spring that their services will not be required at the close of the school year. No reason has to be given. Once a teacher assumes permanent status, however, a district's administration must go through a long, slow due process if a teacher is to be terminated. The termination process is very seldom used, and nearly all permanent teachers end up assured of lifetime employment, steadily increasing compensation, excellent benefits, and the satisfaction of doing work that makes a difference every single day.

In California, teacher movement from one district to another is further discouraged in many districts because only some of a teacher's years of service will be "recognized" for placement on the salary schedule in a new district. And to add a further barrier to movement from one district to another, a teacher's permanent status is only valid in the district in which it was earned, so the teacher who switches districts takes the risk of reverting to probationary status and having to re-earn the permanent status lost as a result of changing school districts. That's a risk most teachers don't want to assume, so the end result is that educators tend to settle into one district and remain there.

As long as one remains a teacher, staying in one school district is to the teacher's benefit. She learns her school and community, forms friendships and partnerships, and has the luxury of stable employment with consistent salary increases. This all works to the teacher's benefit until she wants to move into an administrative position, because few administrative positions come available each year, and competition for those positions is often quite keen.

A second element that makes it difficult for a teacher to get promoted into the administrative ranks within her own district is a by-product of the comfort that comes with working in one place for a long time: colleagues often have a difficult time seeing a great teacher as anything other than just that—a great teacher. A former California State Principal of the Year addressed this phenomenon in a conversation with me when she quoted a passage from the fourth chapter of Luke, in which Jesus says, "Truly I tell you . . . no prophet is accepted in his hometown" (Luke 4:24, NIV).

LESSON 6: GET MENTORS AND GET NETWORKED

An aspiring principal who begins working as an assistant principal has already invested in herself by earning a graduate degree, has likely been an excellent teacher and teacher-leader, and has demonstrated the capacity to work extremely hard. Aspiring principals are highly skilled and motivated. Sometimes these aspiring educational leaders wish to climb into the principal's chair very quickly, seeing their time as an assistant principal as merely a weigh station on the road to bigger things. However, most new assistant principals have no idea how little they really know and how much they still need to learn.

Ironically, the further up an administrator gets promoted during a career, the more she needs to learn in each position in order to be successful. That's where mentors and networking come in. An aspiring principal's first mentor is a crucial person: the principal to whom she reports. If the principal has participated in the hiring of the newly minted assistant principal, then he'll likely be quite invested in her success.

A new assistant principal will have much to learn in her new position, especially if she has switched schools or districts. She'll need to learn about the culture of the school and its community, and how things get done at the site and in the district. She'll need to learn where the proverbial land mines may be buried, who the political players are, and who should be called at the district office to get certain things done. It takes time and some patience to learn these things, but the new administrator is granted some time to learn.

A new assistant principal needs mentors to help her through the myriad of challenges she will encounter for the first time. For instance, when is something considered an emergency? The answer is, it depends (a common answer to many school leadership questions). There are principals who will tell you that an emergency is when someone is injured, bleeding, or not breathing, and that everything else can be given some time before action is taken.

A second key question concerns just how much flexibility our new assistant principal can be expected to exercise. While it's easy to take action in strict accordance with rules and policies, the assistant principal will undoubtedly encounter situations where strict application of the rules results in unintended negative consequences. A famous old saw about this is that school administrators should not let the law get in the way of doing what's right for kids. While this sounds wise, a new assistant principal will need clarity from her mentor before she starts acting in less than perfect accordance with the rules.

It's important for aspiring principals to have mentors who will tell them the truth, which means that an aspiring principal must be emotionally prepared to hear truths that aren't always comfortable. New assistant principals are in a tough spot: they have moved from being stars on their previous campuses, loved by their students, respected by their coworkers, and often blessed with profound influence in matters of curriculum and instruction. They quickly have to face the fact that being an assistant principal is a completely different job than what they have held previously.

They will make mistakes, often for the first time in many years. They are going to do things that make others upset at them. And on top of all these new challenges, new assistant principals are likely to find that they get feedback that is more direct or that may seem more negative than what they had experienced as teachers. Here's the difficult part: that feedback, and how our aspiring principal takes it, are key to her learning and succeeding in her new job.

So who is likely to tell our aspiring principal the truth with the requisite tact, kindness, and encouragement she needs? Some school districts will pair new administrators up with veterans at the district office or at other campuses. It's always good for an aspiring principal to have a mentor with a district-level perspective. The pace of work in a district office is different than at a school site, and our aspiring principal who makes such a connection is likely to discover that a district-level administrator is open to regular conversation.

Another source of mentors can come from the aspiring principal's peer network. It's always a good idea to join the local administrators association because one learns that everyone in school leadership struggles at times. It's wonderful to talk with peers in other districts because, as one learns, there are a myriad of approaches to a given issue in school leadership, and learning how someone else has attacked the problem you're facing can be of great value.

Early in her career, an aspiring principal may find it difficult to reach out and develop many relationships with peers and mentors, but as she soldiers on she will encounter other mentors and better opportunities to network. Many school administrators grow their network by volunteering. Accreditation agencies always need volunteers to serve on visiting teams. Serving on accreditation teams provides a way to expand one's knowledge about effective schools (and less effective ones) while expanding one's network.

Local school administrators' associations are always on the hunt for volunteers. Sometimes just making a phone call or sending an e-mail to the right person in the association can launch an aspiring principal into a greater network and superb learning opportunities. More important, serving an organization makes it easier to call those new friends for counsel when one runs into a challenge.

LESSON 7: UNSTICK YOURSELF TO BECOME A PRINCIPAL

One of the more difficult lessons many an assistant principal endures is the slow-motion realization that she is getting stuck as an assistant principal. Generally speaking, the assistant principal who serves more than five years in a single position can be considered stuck. One way to respond to being stuck is to transfer from one school to another, especially if that transfer involves a change in the school's grade-level configuration or a change of responsibility, such as moving from an assignment focused on discipline to an assignment focused on curriculum and instruction.

It's not at all unusual for assistant principals to begin applying for principal positions after four years, and the stronger candidates who have performed well and have strong recommendations can expect to make it into the interview phase of a principal selection process. Nearly all who become assistant principals do so with one purpose in mind: to get promoted into the position of principal. Failure to promote into a position as a principal can be frustrating, especially since assistant principals have generally been very successful thus far in their careers, having been excellent teachers, having been promoted into administration, and having been given key responsibilities in the operation and leadership of a school.

When an assistant principal is stuck, she has to do something to make change occur. At a certain point, working harder brings precious few benefits to the stuck assistant principal; she merely does more to keep the school running and, ironically, becomes more indispensable *as an assistant principal*. The assistant principal who has worked hard for four years, who has taken on additional work at every turn, and who has received exemplary reviews needs to reach out and do something different in order to be noticed and make her ambitions clear.

That's when it's time to pick up the phone and make some calls. Meet with your mentor, if you have one. Meet with district-level administrators, even the superintendent if possible. The purpose of those meetings is to learn. As you meet with each of these people, ask what you can do to improve your standing so that you might get to the principal's office one day. Ask them for their assessment of your strengths and areas where they think you need to grow. Don't argue with their answers; just ask the questions and listen. You're not there to persuade these people that they've misjudged you; you're there to better understand just what their judgment is. The very act of meeting with these leaders and asking for guidance is likely to have a positive impact on the next school year. Baring your soul and your struggles to those leaders will cause them to look at you differently. That series of discussions is a good start to getting unstuck.

The second part of getting unstuck might come as a surprise. Besides learning about how others are assessing you, it's important to get some coaching if you intend to unstick yourself. While this is a common practice in the business world, it's an uncommon practice in school administration. It may be hard to find anyone in your area who is doing that kind of work with school administrators, so this step may require some persistence.

Ask leaders in your district and region to whom you might turn for coaching. If they come up with no recommendations, look for someone involved in executive coaching in the business world. Keep working at this until you find someone with whom you're comfortable, who has experience, and whose services you can afford. Yes, expect to pay, but this in an investment in yourself; you'll be a better candidate for promotion once you make this commitment.

LESSON 8: CREATE SUPERB PAPERS

In California, the process for selecting administrators begins with documents. Back in the day, one literally put together packets of papers that contained a resume, letters of recommendation, transcripts, and a cover letter. In time, the process moved from actual pieces of paper to PDFs submitted via an electronic network called EDJOIN, which started in California and now serves 20 states. Even though the medium has changed, the process still begins with words on a page, so it is essential that a prospective principal creates superb papers that will stand out enough to earn the candidate an interview.

First, let's get the technical element of "papers" out of the way. While EDJOIN and other services accept a variety of document formats, these services are very clear upfront about what they want to see: PDFs. Hiring agents want to see PDFs because the format ends up proving consistent; it is easy to work with, and it ends up displaying things on the reader's page just as they are displayed when created.

EDJOIN has been in use for teacher hiring for many years, and too many times screening committees get stuck trying to read a submission by a teacher candidate (in a format other than PDF) that requires them to zoom in (or out) and occasionally to rotate the document (onscreen!) just to see it. The person reading over your online submission is going to look at hundreds of pages through their computer screen during an administrative recruitment, so it behooves you to keep your documents clear, neat, right-side up, properly zoomed, and in the preferred format.

Second, make sure anything you scan into PDF form is easy to read. This can be problematic with transcripts since they are often printed on challenging kinds of paper. You may need to find a professional service to help you make your documents look great. Bottom line: take time to ensure that your documents look as good as possible. As table 2.1 shows, applicants should group their various documents into a few files rather than submitting them all as separate files. Ask yourself this question: If you were a district administrator reading 100 application packets for a principal position, which of these two batches of documents would you prefer to read?

Of course a hiring committee would rather read the package submitted by the first candidate. All the files are in the same desirable PDF format. The fact that the documents have been organized by type and that they are so clearly labeled leaves a strong first impression that the candidate is organized, thoughtful, and attends to detail. These are good qualities for a principal to possess, and it is wise to communicate those qualities immediately.

A candidate for the position of principal controls three kinds of documents in her packet: her cover letter, her resume, and her letters of recommendation. The first document in any application packet is the cover letter, and even though it can feel pretty generic, one should think of it like the suit worn to an interview: it leaves a valuable first impression. Hiring committees everywhere encounter cover letters with errors in spelling, grammar, and punctuation. Yes—spelling errors. Since school leadership

Table 2.1. Application Documents Submitted by Two Candidates

Candidate 1 Files	Candidate 2 Files
Coverletter.PDF	Coverletter.doc
Resume.PDF	Resume.doc
Recommendations.PDF	SmithRecommendation.PDF
Credentials.PDF	JonesRecommendation.PDF
Transcripts.PDF	OrtizRecommendation.PDF
	EnglishCredential.PDF
	AdminCredential.PDF
	UCIundergrad transcript.PDF
	UCIMAtranscript.PDF

depends so heavily on one's ability to use the English language well, you'd think candidates would not make these kinds of mistakes—which is exactly what the human resource officer thinks when reviewing 100 of these! A quality cover letter will include the following characteristics:

1. It will use clear, direct language. In the famous words of Strunk and White in *The Elements of Style*, a cover letter will "use less words."
2. It will be addressed to the right person. "To Whom It May Concern" is not the right person. The name of the district is not the right person. These days, vacancy postings for principal positions will usually include the name of the person to whom correspondence should be addressed. When in doubt, it is an appropriate practice to address the letter to the Assistant Superintendent, Human Resources.
3. The letter will not say, "My name is . . ." Don't waste your words on that.
4. A good cover letter demonstrates that the candidate has the ability to form sentences, and it leaves an impression, however brief, on the reader. The better candidates know what impression they want the human resources officer to feel after reading their cover letter.

As an example, figure 2.1 shows the cover letter I submitted to the Alvord Unified School District in 2006 when I was selected to be the principal of La Sierra High School.

Several things are communicated in this cover letter. It leads with one clear sentence about being driven to improve student performance. It communicates an understanding of the bigger picture of a principal's job. It is easy to read, is short, uses a legible font, and doesn't try to say too much.

Cover letters are invariably followed by resumes in administrative applications. A quality resume takes time to put together. In administrative hiring, a resume needs to clearly communicate the candidate's education and training, work history, and specific responsibilities. It must be readable, and it should provide some visual cues about the candidate. Figure 2.2 shows the complete resume I submitted back in 2006.

At the time this resume was submitted, it stood out for a number of reasons. It was longer than recommended, the standard wisdom of the day being that a resume should be short, one page if possible. The inclusion of excerpts from recommendations proved attention-getting for the time period. The resume lists the work done with enough detail to create a picture of excellence at work. Using bullet points instead of longer narratives keeps things simple. A block paragraph about one's work at a school is difficult to read and decode in a resume; bullet points are simpler for most readers.

Robert F. Cunard, Ed.D.
My Street
My City, State, Zip

May 21, 2006

Suzanne M. Pickup, Ed.D.
Assistant Superintendent, Personnel
Alvord Unified School District

Dear Dr. Pickup:

I am an educational leader driven to improve student performance. I believe that all students can achieve the academic challenges of the California Content Standards. The mission of the high school principal is to promote that belief to a school and community, to motivate, equip and support teachers to attain that goal, and to celebrate the accomplishments of the students, their families, and the school in reaching their dreams.

To insure that all students achieve, the principal must promote a culture of success for all. For too long, we have accepted the notion that only some students really belong in universities. My involvement in AVID and Puente and other outreach programs with UC Irvine provide me with clear and convincing evidence that all students have a place in the university. But the deep structure of large high schools often makes it difficult for some students and families to find the kind of connection with the school many students need in order to achieve. To motivate those students, the principal and the faculty must work together to find ways to make a big school small and to better connect students and families to school.

I am proud to have been a leader in supporting, developing, and designing systems which have better connected students to school. I have fostered partnerships with colleges and universities, promoted AVID, developed a Puente Program, and designed and implemented a small learning community redesign of Newport Harbor High School. I have done these things because I have continually looked for ways to improve student opportunity to learn. But most of all, I do this work because what we're doing in high schools—even a high school as successful as the California Distinguished School where I presently work—isn't yet enough to insure that all students can achieve their dreams.

Sincerely,

Robert F. Cunard

Figure 2.1.

Robert F. Cunard

XXXXX My Street
Mission Viejo, CA 92691
(XXX) XXX-XXXX **(C)**
(XXX) XXX-XXXX **(O)**
rcunard@email

"Robert infuses a sense of empathy that is a pleasure to witness...Robert has been able to reach out and touch all levels of the community in a manner that has impressed many. Robert..."gets it done!"...The sheer volume of what he is able to effectively deal with at any given time, no matter what the stress level, is most impressive. He is incredibly task-oriented and infuses a high degree of care, attention, and professionalism to every project he assumes."

**M.V.
Principal
Newport Harbor High**

Oct. 2003 - Present	**Assistant Principal** **Newport Harbor High School** **Newport-Mesa Unified School District** <ul><li>Counseling and Master Schedule</li><li>WASC Self-Study Coordinator</li><li>California Distinguished School Application Primary Author</li><li>Smaller Learning Communities Federal Grant: Primary Author</li><li>Curriculum Alignment Project Design and Supervision</li><li>Professional Development</li><li>Technology</li><li>Facilities Modernization</li><li>Athletics and Activities</li><li>District English Curriculum Committee</li></ul>
July 2001 - Sept. 2003	**Assistant Principal** **Estancia High School** **Newport-Mesa Unified School District** <ul><li>Founder of Puente Program</li><li>Founder of School-wide Character Education Program</li><li>Counseling and Guidance</li><li>Wrote NMUSD High School Exit Examination Remediation Course</li><li>AVID Supervisor</li><li>English Language Development program, and formation of ELAC</li><li>Student Discipline and School Safety</li><li>Facilities and Operations</li></ul>
July 1997 - June 2001	**Assistant Principal** **Corona del Mar Middle/High School** **Newport-Mesa Unified School District** <ul><li>Digital High School program</li><li>Site Budget</li><li>Athletics and Activities</li><li>Facilities and Operations</li><li>Student Discipline and School Safety</li><li>Commencement and Senior Activities</li><li>Booster Club Liaison</li></ul>

Figure 2.2.

> "I have found him to be creative and innovative in his approach to situations and I believe his ability to make confident decisions will be a trait that will assist him in all the decisions that face a High School Principal."
>
> **M.A., Ed.D**
> **Director of Assessment**
> **Newport-Mesa Unified**

> "He visits classrooms regularly, sees the effectiveness and needs of our instructional program insightfully, and promotes positive change...I have come to trust and rely on his advice. He is well read on and clearly understands educational issues."
>
> **T.A., Ed.D.**
> **Principal**
> **Estancia High School**

June 1993 - **Activities Director**
June 1997 **Irvine High School**
     Irvine Unified School District
- Coordination of all Student Activities
- Academic Awards Programs
- Commencement Ceremonies
- Facilities Use and School Calendar
- Co-Author, SB 1274 Grant
- Boys Varsity Tennis Coach

Sept. 1989 - **English Teacher, Mentor Teacher**
June 1997 **Irvine High School**
     Irvine Unified School District
- Designed and implemented district-wide staff development on performance-based assessment
- Taught English courses ranging from ninth through eleventh grades
- Developed curriculum for ninth grade at-risk courses
- Developed tenth grade English and European History interdisciplinary course
- Master teacher

Sept. 1985 - **English Teacher, Mentor Teacher**
June 1989 **Lakewood High School**
     Long Beach Unified School District
- Taught tenth and eleventh grade English at both college preparatory and remedial levels
- Mentor teacher with emphasis on new teacher support.
- Redesigned tenth grade English curriculum.
- Master teacher.
- Girls Junior Varsity Basketball Coach.

Sept 1982 - **English Teacher**
June 1985 **Washington Junior High**
     Long Beach Unified School District
- Taught English and reading
- Boys Basketball Coach.

Figure 2.2. *Continued*

> "He has a well-developed professional philosophy and is undaunted by the ambiguities and complexities of leadership... he is smart and he has a true commitment to doing what is best for students."
>
> **D.E., Ed.D.**
> **UCI Credential Programs**

> "He is extremely bright and is an excellent communicator, both orally and in writing...People like working with Robert. He is a good listener...Dr. Cunard works very well with faculty, students, parents, and district leaders. I have witnessed his ability to exercise good judgment.."
>
> **T.J.,**
> **Assistant**
> **Superintendent**
> **Newport-Mesa Unified**
> **School District, Retired**

EDUCATION

Sept 1977 - **University of California at Berkeley**
June 1981   B.A. - Rhetoric

Sept 1981 - **University of California at Irvine**
June 1982   Teaching Credential, Secondary English

Jan 1984 - **Cal State University Long Beach**
May 1986   M.A. - Educational Administration

Sept 1986 - **Pepperdine University**
May 1993   Ed. D. - Institutional Management

Aug 1998 - **University of California, Irvine**
June 1999   Tier II Credential Program

CREDENTIALS

- **Tier II Administrative Services**
- **Clear Ryan Single Subject, English**

ORGANIZATIONS

- **ACSA, Phi Delta Kappa, ASCD**

REFERENCES

Mr. M.V.
Principal, Newport Harbor High School
(XXX) XXX-XXXX

Dr. M.A.
Director of Assessment
Newport-Mesa Unified School District
(XXX) XXX-XXXX

Dr. F.N.
Director of Secondary Curriculum and Instruction
Newport-Mesa Unified School District
(XXX) XXX-XXXX

Figure 2.2.   *Continued*

A resume, like everything else in your packet, is a document for others, not for you. It should be built to address the needs of the reader—who will read a hundred of them over the course of a day or two once it comes time to winnow down a field for interviews.

It surprises people that the candidate controls the recommendations written by others, but the best candidates actually do control them. Here's how they do it: the best principal candidates work very hard in their jobs, achieve their objectives, do far more than the minimum, and build relationships with a variety of people in their organization so that when they ask for recommendations *they know exactly what those recommendations will say*. So even though the candidate doesn't actually write the recommendations submitted on her behalf, she really does control what goes into them.

Another important element of recommendation control has to do with who the candidate recruits to write those recommendations. In California, it's typical in a principal recruitment that candidates provide three recommendations, and at least one is supposed to be from the candidate's direct supervisor. Hiring committees tend to appreciate those applicants, both teaching and administrative, who go beyond the minimum and provide more than three recommendations. A suggestion is to bundle all your recommendations into one PDF, with the most current, most important recommendations first. Many hiring officers enjoy reading extra recommendations because they give a clearer picture of the candidate.

There is one final piece of wisdom regarding the recommendation process: motivated hiring officers will telephone people who the candidate has not listed in their resume nor who have written recommendations. At first that may seem a little unfair, but put yourself in the hiring officer's shoes, and you can soon see why this is a good strategy. It's common in principal selection processes for hiring officers to call people they know and trust in an effort to learn more about a candidate. Given the importance of a principal's job, this makes perfect sense.

This will work in the candidate's favor so long as the candidate has a strong track record and has remained focused on relationships. Since the successful principal must be a relationship builder, these back-channel phone calls are not an unfair part of the process; indeed, they may be essential. The point here is obvious: the successful principal candidate is one who is going to get great reviews from everyone.

LESSON 9: INVEST IN YOUR SELECTION SKILLS

Once you've done your work well for several years and established a reputation of excellence, and once you've put together great papers, you need to be able to back those papers up with skills and wisdom when you are selected for an interview. Unfortunately, many get stuck as assistant principals because they have not developed the right kind of skills to enable them to stand out in the interview process. That's where mentors and coaching come in.

Executive coaches in the private sector know that the best candidates know themselves well, and their starting point in coaching a client is often a new self-assessment. One assessment used in executive coaching is based on the Myers-Briggs personality inventory. These days, you can find the assessment and take it for free just by visiting https://www.mbtionline.com/. A follow-up on the results of that assessment often reveals strengths and potential weaknesses that may emerge during a selection process.

In addition to having clear self-knowledge, many principal candidates make a serious mistake: they don't answer interview questions properly! This can be terribly embarrassing to the aspiring principal; how could she be answering questions improperly? She is experienced, smart, and detail oriented! What isn't there to love about her answers? Simply put, many candidates make the same two fatal errors over and over: their answers are too long and detailed, and they fail to focus on the right things in those answers. Too many aspiring principals treat interviews like TV quiz shows, doing their very best to get every element of every question meticulously answered. That's a terrible mistake, and the stuck assistant principal will have to learn how to break out of that habit.

Administrative interviews are designed to get the interviewee talking, telling stories. Every response to a question about one's prior leadership work has three parts: the situation, the actions you took, and the results. The overriding terrible mistake—and a mistake commonly made in administrative interviews—is in not allocating response time properly. The best responses describe the situation as briefly as possible, spend just a little more time on the actions taken, *and spend the largest amount of time on the results.*

Many candidates answer questions backwards, spending way too much time on the situation, too much time on the details of what they have done, and not nearly enough time on the impact. When you're being considered to lead a school, it's the *impact* of your actions that matters most, not the subtle brilliance of what you did. If the committee wants to know more about your brilliant strategic details, they'll follow up during the interview—or later. Table 2.2 offers an illustration of two ways to answer a question.

Before coaching, many candidates answer the question with Response 1, reveling in the details and minutiae of the challenge faced. Even though everything in Response 1 is correct and reflects what was actually done,

Table 2.2. Two Ways to Answer an Interview Question

Question: Tell us about a time when your leadership improved student academic achievement.

	Response 1	Response 2
Situation	While working as an A.P. at XYZ High School, I was asked to lead our site's response to a disastrous review of our program for English Language Learners. The school was swept up into a Comité de los Padres sanction, and we were put under the microscope of the CDE for two years. It was a really disruptive time, with a new EL director being installed at the district, and we all had to undergo a lot of training and development about how our program for ELLs needed to change.	At XYZ High School, I was asked to improve our program for English Language Learners after an unsatisfactory state review.
Action	The new district director and I met several times. We formed a committee at school, which included teachers, parents, and students. We went over our results and the state report. We did a lot of data analysis about our ELLs and how they were doing in history, science, and math. We also looked deeply at how many of our ELLs were reclassifying as fluent in English. We visited schools with better programs for ELLs. We ended up redesigning the schedule for ELLs, moving many of them out of sheltered classes and into mainstream classes. To support them, we had to find ways to get the ELD teacher to serve as a co-teacher in other subjects, which was challenging. Finally, we designed and implemented a half-day professional development workshop for all teachers at XYZ about ELLs, their needs, the state requirements for their program, and several best practices they could use in their classrooms to help ELLs improve their skills.	Working with our new district director, I formed a task force at the school, which included teachers, parents, and several students. We studied the state review, and learned about best practices in EL programs. We put together professional development for our entire faculty, and we began to mainstream ELLs into core content classes instead of keeping them in sheltered courses.
Result	The next year our reclassification rate for ELLs improved by 10% over prior year results.	The following year, our ELLs improved their pass rates in science, social science, and math by an average of 15%. Their performance on our internal reading assessments showed strong growth, with the average ELL growing by an effect size of .5 in one year. Also in that next year, our ELLs improved their reclassification rate as Fluent English Speakers by 10% over prior year results.

it's a lousy answer because it's poorly focused. Even worse, Response 1 buries some really important information about the academic results students attained after the improved program was put in place! Why might Response 1 leave out that information? The interviewee who spends a lot of time on the situation and the actions taken often runs out of time to discuss the results in any detail.

Learning how to better handle oneself in interviews makes a huge difference. The candidate is still the same person, the same administrator, but now she knows how to communicate her achievements more effectively. She'll also better prepare for interviews. Less savvy candidates spend too much time preparing for an interview by primarily studying the school and district that is interviewing. Too many candidates strive to memorize their student achievement data in the belief that being conversant about this provides some sort of advantage in the interview.

After coaching, wiser candidates spend far less time studying schools and districts, and far more time studying themselves and working to fashion a vision of who they are and how they might go about doing their work if selected to serve as the next principal. The best interviewees know what they want to communicate about themselves during an interview, and they find ways to communicate those specific things, regardless of what the interview questions might be. It's hard to do that if one treats an interview as a quiz show. When your interview preparation becomes more focused on yourself and what you want to communicate, interviewing becomes easier and less stressful—though certainly not less work.

LESSON 10: KEEP YOUR HEAD UP—IT'S NOT ABOUT YOU

If it isn't already obvious, it must be stated directly that it is very difficult to be selected to serve as a principal. After getting an assistant principal job, the universe may get even with you later. There aren't very many principals compared to assistant principals, and nearly all assistant principals wish to be promoted into a principal's position. This can be a really frustrating time for aspiring principals. Multiple rejections (the way most unsuccessful candidates view their non-selections) are not easy to take.

It is challenging to accept the notion that one isn't getting those jobs because one simply isn't the best candidate. Period. No matter one's skills and work ethic, it is terribly frustrating that hiring committees all over your region think differently. It will take some direct, challenging conversations with mentors, coaches, and friends to help the aspiring principal through that, and it may take time, effort, and an investment to get unstuck, move out of a rut, and finally break through. But never doubt that it is, indeed, possible to do just that.

IN MY EXPERIENCE
If They Don't Want You

After four years serving as the principal of La Sierra High School, I put myself through principal selections once again, hoping to secure a principalship close to my home in Orange County. A strong district in Orange County began a recruitment for two high school principals early in the spring season, and I was all over it. I had a great first interview, and the superintendent telephoned me that afternoon, personally inviting me back to meet with him and telling me that he was expecting to introduce me at one of his two high schools as their next principal the following Friday. I was ecstatic.

Five days later when I came in for that second interview, what I thought would be my benediction, it was immediately clear that something had changed. The superintendent interviewed me from behind his huge desk while I sat in a short chair. The questions I got were sharp and pointed, and it was clear within moments that I was not going to meet the faculty at any of his schools two days hence. The miserable interview concluded after thirty minutes when he said, "We're bringing in another candidate." That was that; I was out.

It hurt—until a couple of weeks later when I had occasion to meet with Jim, a retired administrator from that Orange County district who was assigned to work with La Sierra on our upcoming accreditation process. We got to talking, and I told him my story. When I finished, he told me something that I came to realize was just brilliant in its simplicity, "If they don't want you, then you don't want them." For some reason, it was as if the clouds parted at that moment and down shone a nugget of revealed wisdom. Jim was absolutely right. Why would I want to work for an organization that had moved on, that didn't want me?

I started to review all the times in my career when someone else had been selected principal over me (there were many). To me, all those non-selections were failures. What I hadn't realized is that they weren't failures; they simply weren't matches. I wasn't failing when I wasn't selected; I just hadn't met the right people and the right circumstances—yet. Furthermore, the more I looked around me, the more I discovered what I should have known all along: everyone who gets interviewed is qualified to be a principal, and being smarter, or more hardworking, or even taller or better dressed really doesn't matter very much. What matters is often intangible.

A couple of weeks after Jim revealed his nugget of wisdom, I had another interview in Orange County. I nailed it, walking out believing that I had given absolutely my best interview ever. And I wasn't invited back—again. I took this one better, though (thanks, Jim), and watched with interest over the years as the candidate that district selected proved very successful in that principalship, ultimately being selected Orange County's Secondary Principal of the Year five years later. Obviously, he was the right fit for that school and community.

> *Could I have done the job? Sure, but so could everyone else who was interviewed. I just wasn't the best fit. The selection committee did me and that school a favor by making the choice they made. As it happens, a few weeks later I did prove to be the right fit to become the principal at Magnolia High School in Anaheim, and six years later, I, too, ended up selected as Orange County's Secondary Principal of the Year.*

CHAPTER 2 KEY POINTS AND STRATEGIES

1. Don't take shortcuts on the pathway to the principalship. Do the work.
2. Do all your work with excellence. Expect to go above and beyond the norm in each position you hold if you want to become a principal.
3. Everyone you work with becomes a potential reference. Everyone.
4. Continually invest in your own learning.
5. In a profession where many stay rooted to one place for an entire career, the aspiring principal should expect to move.
6. Get mentors early on, and be a mentor to others. Network, even if you think you're never leaving your present district.
7. Have the courage to unstick yourself, should it prove necessary.
8. Create great papers and always consider the reality of your reader.
9. If necessary, invest in your selection skills.
10. If they don't want you, then you don't want them.

Three

The New Principal

"Well," said Pooh, "what I like best," and then he had to stop and think. Because although Eating Honey was a very good thing to do, there was a moment just before you began to eat it which was better than when you were, but he didn't know what it was called.—A. A. Milne

A rock pile ceases to be a rock pile the moment a single man contemplates it, bearing within him the image of a cathedral.—Antoine de Saint-Exupéry

The new principal faces a number of daunting challenges that arrive quickly; among them are the following:

1. There is a staff of anywhere from 30 to 200 anxious to meet the principal.
2. The new principal often encounters important work that simply must be done in order to open school.
3. The new principal must quickly learn about the school, the district, the community, and how things get done.
4. The new principal is frequently required to make decisions very early on, often with imperfect information.
5. The new principal is inspected, talked about, and second-guessed to a greater degree in the first few months than will ever occur again during her tenure at the site.

These are difficult working conditions, fraught with traps, but the principal must work through them as well as possible and open school well; failure in these first few weeks is simply not an option if one intends to be a successful principal. First impressions in a selection process are important for the selected principal; first impressions on the job for the new principal are important for an entire community.

During the first six months, the new principal should expect to work longer and harder than at any time in her career to ensure that school really does open well and that the right first impressions are made. Bad beginnings are rarely forgiven, particularly since schoolteachers tend to have very long memories. About being new, Richard DuFour used to say in his presentations, "Win small, win early, win often." The new principal is wise to heed DuFour's advice. Fortunately, there are things the new principal can do to ensure that she does win early on and set a foundation for future wins.

BEING THE PRINCIPAL IS A DIFFERENT JOB

One of the most challenging aspects of being a new principal is that he must realize that the principal's job is entirely different than any prior job he has held in the pathway. A new principal is frequently tempted to demonstrate his skills early on in the job by taking on a piece of work that truly belongs to others. The temptation is there because the new principal wants to demonstrate his competence, to set an example of what quality work looks like so that others will follow that example in the future. In some cases—where there has clearly been incompetence—taking on someone else's task may be necessary, but most of the time when the new principal does someone else's work, he ends up unintentionally communicating his disrespect of the very teammates in the school on whom he'll have to depend!

The new principal will certainly have a number of managerial functions to perform during the first six months as a new, improved order is established. Table 3.1 illustrates seventeen differences between leading, managing, and it's a good idea to keep these seventeen things in mind from time to time. The principal who ends up spending most of her time involved in activities on the left hand side of the chart will find it difficult to sustain improvement in student academic achievement.

POWER AND THE PRINCIPAL

The new principal picks up a number of heady responsibilities. She can hire people. She can discipline employees; in rare occasions, she can terminate employees. She assumes responsibility for public funds, and for the first time ever in a career, she can spend public money just using her signature. (In my final year as principal in 2015–2016, the combined value of the budgets I supervised and spent funds from exceeded one million dollars.) There are other powers as well, including the power to assign a teacher her schedule of classes or her students, as well as her classroom. In addition to these formal powers, the principal often develops and exercises informal powers over time.

But before the new principal goes to work exercising her powers, she would be well advised to stop, take a few breaths, and heed the advice of

> ### IN MY EXPERIENCE
> ### Don't Butt In
>
> I was fortunate to learn this lesson in the first few days when I was the new principal at La Sierra. Motivated by the very best of intentions, I intervened in something my administrative assistant was doing. To her immense credit, Jamie simmered through the afternoon and evening about this little (to me) thing, and she made a decision to discuss it first thing the next morning. During our morning meeting, she waited until the end when I asked if there was anything else, and that's when she said there was.
>
> Clearly, directly, and with just a hint of force, she took me back to my intervention of the previous afternoon, and she told me she wished I hadn't done it. Jamie was proud of her skills and her ability to make our school run smoothly. There would be plenty of things to come in our years ahead that she would happily hand off to me, but she wanted to do the work that she knew she was capable of doing. She wanted to help people and solve problems, and she told me in the clearest and kindest terms that our school would run much better if all the other employees took similar levels of ownership and used their skills to solve problems. If I jumped in all the time, why would they continue to exercise initiative?
>
> Jamie and I only had that talk one time, ever, but it proved one of the most powerful discussions we ever had during our years together. I had just finished serving nine years as an assistant principal, and it had been my job to solve problems; everything that landed on my desk or in my office required my personal intervention. That's what assistant principals do.
>
> Assistant principals are managers, and they are critical to making schools work. Sometimes, assistant principals function as leaders, but most of their functions are managerial. Principals, on the other hand, are leaders, and being a leader is a different job. I love the old saying "managers steer the ship, and the leader decides where it will go." Recently, I came across a more fully developed document published by Resourceful Manager (2016), which illustrates 17 differences between managers and leaders (see table 3.1).
>
> (continued)

Table 3.1. Managers versus Leaders: 17 Differences

A Manager . . .	A Leader . . .
• Tells	• Sells
• Plans the details	• Sets the direction
• Minimizes risks	• Takes risks
• Instructs employees	• Encourages people
• Has objectives	• Has vision
• Meets expectations	• Charts new growth
• Eyes the bottom line	• Eyes the horizon
• Accepts the status quo	• Challenges the status quo
• Sees a problem	• Sees an opportunity
• Thinks short term	• Thinks long term
• Follows the map	• Carves new roads
• Approves	• Motivates
• Establishes rules	• Breaks rules
• Assigns duties	• Fosters ideas
• Votes with their head	• Votes with their heart
• Relies on control	• Inspires trust
• Does things right	• Does the right thing

John Black and Fenwick English, whose classic text, *What They Don't Tell You in Schools of Education about School Administration* (2001), is the best I've ever read about the position of the principal and the context of her power. Of new principals, Fenwick and English wrote:

> Nothing in their training addressed the fact that once classroom teachers cross the threshold of their classroom doors and leave the classroom for administration, they all but leave the field of education and enter a new field altogether—the field of politics. . . . The rules of the game are different and, for the most part, *are unwritten*. (Black and English, 2001, p. x)

The new principal faces an interesting conundrum: she has made it through a grueling selection process, is eagerly anticipated by a school and community, may be coming into a school facing real challenges (as I was each time), but the standard advice she is most likely to receive is to sit tight and spend her first year just steering the ship—managing it.

ENTRY PLANNING

In order to be successful and be able to exercise power effectively, the new principal must develop an understanding and appreciation of the school, the district, and the community. As Black and English (2001) note, "School administration involves knowing the territory.... The traditions of the schools are its territory. Understanding that tradition is the territory is the first job of the radical who wants to change any organization and the way it functions" (p. 8). In recent years, new principals have begun to use entry planning, a tool from the business world, to systematically speed up the process of building relationships and better understanding the territory in a new school. An entry plan that is well publicized and adhered to by a new principal will do many things to help her become a successful principal:

1. A published entry plan demonstrates that the new principal actually has a plan for meeting everyone and for learning about the territory in the new school.
2. A published entry plan immediately answers the question so many ask about a new principal—namely, "What is she doing all day long?"
3. An entry plan is a great vehicle for structuring a new principal's work for the first six months.
4. A published entry plan buys the new principal time to learn the territory before making decisions.
5. A published entry plan, if faithfully implemented and reported out, models the new principal's high-quality work processes and sets the stage for thoughtful practices and decision making in the future.
6. A published entry plan, well executed and reported, is an easy early win for the new principal.

Given all these benefits, you'd expect that all new principals would be designing entry plans, publishing them, implementing them, and then reporting on them. But that's not true, and the reason is simple: entry planning is a lot of work and takes nearly all the new principal's time during her first six months. And, of course, once school begins, the daily routines of school can quickly become all encompassing, thus sabotaging the best intentions of a published entry plan.

Despite these challenges, the process will serve principals well. Once appointed to the position, principals may share details of the proposed entry plan with the superintendent before publishing it to the school and district staff affected by the entry plan. As an example, figure 3.1 shows the plan I published when I became the principal of Magnolia High School in 2010, which is available at http://www.thesuccessfulprincipal.org/entry-planning.html.

Robert F. Cunard
Entry Plan
Magnolia High School Principalship

Preface

The purpose of an Entry Plan is to insure that a leader in a new school systematically and collaboratively learns about the school, its community, its systems and processes, and—most importantly—the people in the organization.

Goals

This plan aims to achieve the following goals:

1. To introduce me to the Magnolia community
2. To meet with key personnel in the Magnolia community and to develop an understanding of their hopes and dreams for Magnolia
3. To develop an effective collaborative relationship with Magnolia leadership
4. To develop an understanding of 'how things get done' at Magnolia and within the Anaheim Union High School District
5. To study student academic performance at Magnolia
6. To understand the areas of strength at Magnolia
7. To understand where Magnolia can and should focus improvement efforts
8. To report the findings of the Entry Plan

Activities

During my first 100 days at Magnolia, I expect to be engaged in a number of specific activities, which will include:

- Reading and research
- Structured interviews
- Public appearances
- Classroom observations

Figure 3.1.

- Writing and reporting out

Reading and Research

I would like to begin as quickly as possible to read and review the following:

- AUHSD Board Policies and Administrative Regulations
- MHS student achievement data
    - STAR results
    - CAHSEE results
    - A.P. results
    - API and AYP data
    - CELDT results
- The ASTA contract
- The APGA contract
- The CSEA contract
- The AFSCME contract
- Magnolia's last two WASC Self-Studies
- Magnolia's last two Single School Plans
- Magnolia's site budget
- Magnolia's master schedule
- Any Magnolia grant/award applications in the last three years
- Yearbooks for the last 10 years

Structured Interviews

I will invite all staff to meet with me individually. At a minimum, I will conduct structured interviews with the following:

Site Staff

Denise Selbe (former principal)
Eva Valencia (sole returning assistant principal)
Lorena Dayton (activities director)
Steve Gonzalez (head counselor)
Sharon Yager (Principal's administrative assistant)
Carlos Rosas (Plant Manager)
Department Chairs
Greg Chastain (Outgoing Athletic Director)
Sara Galasso (Site Technology Lead teacher)

District Staff

Fred Navarro (Assistant Superintendent - Education)
Russell Lee-Sung (Assistant Superintendent - Human Resources)

Figure 3.1. *Continued*

Tim Holcomb (Deputy Superintendent - Operations)
Diane Poore (Assistant Superintendent - Business Services)
Susan Stocks (Director - Categorical Programs)
Judy Bright (Coordinator - Assessment)
Mike Matsuda (Coordinator - Professional Development)
Rick Martens (Director - Student Services)
Barbara Moore (Director - Special Youth Services)
Cheryl Quadrelli-Jones (Coordinator - Special Programs)
Other High School principals
Feeder MS Principals

Students

Top 20 seniors by GPA
20 seniors at-risk
Captains of athletic teams
Student Council
Club presidents

Community

PTA President
Site Council Parents
ELAC parents
Booster Club leaders

Appearances and Visibility

It's important to be seen publicly to be the principal of Magnolia. There is also an opportunity through appearances to advance the academic mission of Magnolia. I intend to accomplish these goals by doing several things:

- Visiting and observing every teacher in class during the first two weeks of school

- Recognizing academic excellence as a priority through whatever means possible.

- Observing at least one athletic event in every sport, every level, every season.

- Attending concerts and performances by all MHS performing groups.

Writing and Reporting Out

I will use writing as an important part of my communication strategy. I intend to:

- Quickly provide a new principal's statement and photograph for the school website.

- Publish a weekly "Friday Letter" to the Magnolia staff.

- Communicate in writing to the community through our website at least once per month.

- Write a summary of my observations and activities in this entry plan and deliver it the Superintendent and the Magnolia Staff by the start of the second semester.

Figure 3.1. *Continued*

As you can see, this entry plan created quite a few commitments for me as a new principal. The work I committed to do was not different from what all new principals end up doing, but writing it down, publishing it, and then promising to report on what I had learned after one semester raised the stakes considerably. It would have been much less risky to just share the plan with the superintendent and then go about doing it, avoiding the risks of publishing—and failing to get everything done. But being the principal is about leadership, about making commitments and following through on them, and it was important to me to demonstrate that I was willing to do just that.

IN MY EXPERIENCE
The Entry Planning Process

One of the more radical commitments I made in the entry plan right from the start was that I would write to the staff and community regularly, putting out a letter every Friday. Again, it was a bit of a risk to make that commitment because it's so easy to fail to write, but it was important to me to make that commitment and to follow through with it. For the ten years I was a principal, I never missed publishing a letter on Friday morning.

Once the entry plan was published, I set about getting the work done. Since most of the entry plan was about meeting a lot of people, it was important to have a strategy for setting up those meetings, documenting them, and then making sense of all the input. I made up a simple template that I used as the starting point for every conversation I had (see the website). Then came the matter of scheduling all those conversations, and that is where my assistant proved invaluable. We sat down and looked over the list of people called out in the plan, and Jamie started scheduling meetings—dozens of them.

Sometimes I met with people in my office. Sometimes I traveled to the offices of others. I bought a lot of lunches for people. Because I knew myself pretty well and knew that my introverted nature could only handle so many meetings each day, we spaced them out, doing meetings in the mornings, and leaving afternoons and evenings for the reading and research the entry plan called for. For most meetings, I took notes during the conversation, but that wasn't always possible or appropriate, especially if the meeting was a lunch date. For those meetings, I made a point of recording notes as soon after the meeting as possible. I knew I wanted notes, and I was very faithful in keeping up with them.

By the time it was December, I had met with everyone on that original list, and it became time to transition from meeting people and collecting data to the work of distilling all the data into something that would make sense. At

(continued)

> both La Sierra and Magnolia, I took a two-step approach to sharing my findings: I reported them in a Friday letter, and I made a PowerPoint presentation to the staff during a faculty meeting. (All my Friday letters are archived at www.thesuccessfulprincipal.org, and the slides I shared with the Magnolia faculty are available there as well.)
>
> By the time I completed and presented those documents, I had gotten to know both schools pretty well; it was not difficult to identify what we needed to be working on in order to improve. The fact that I chose to publicly identify those issues as well as what I thought we needed to do next actually violated the old adage that a new principal should spend the entire first school year just watching. I thought long and hard about taking that step, but waiting another six months to talk about what we should do next would have had the effect of delaying innovations and improvements until the third year of my principalship, and that was simply too long to wait.
>
> Why should a freshman in a struggling school have to wait until her junior year to benefit from an improved school? And that proved to be one of the nice surprises of the entry plan: while it forced me to go a little slowly and to stay focused on meeting and understanding people, their territory, and the school's gifts and challenges, it ended up providing me with a very solid foundation for taking action more quickly. As the saying goes, sometimes you have to go slow in order to go fast.

YOU AND YOUR ADMINISTRATIVE ASSISTANT—YOUR INDISPENSABLE BEST FRIEND

Once the new principal arrives at school to start that very first day, his administrative assistant will be the first person he meets, and that relationship will become critical in the years ahead if the principal is to be successful. The administrative assistant is the filter for the new principal in myriad ways.

One important role the administrative assistant ends up playing is that he or she very quickly ends up reflecting to the existing staff and community just who the new principal is. Think about it: dozens of people are interested in who their new principal is and what he's like, but since most of these transitions occur during the summer when the vast majority of a school's staff are not working, they end up on the phone with the administrative assistant. They ask questions, and a few curious ones might stop in at the office, ostensibly to check their mail or the condition of their classroom. In my experience, though, what they really wanted to do was learn about the new principal. The next time you're in a school undergoing a principal transition, watch for this; it happens every time.

Over the course of a principal's tenure in a school, his administrative assistant will be there for everything—and I mean everything. They'll see how you act during a crisis. If you talk favorably or unfavorably about others, they'll know. They'll know if you're an encourager, a micro-manager, kind, or vain. They'll come to know how you treat your spouse, your children, and your family. They'll see you at your best, and they'll probably see you at your worst—whether you let them in to those moments or not.

Some principals choose to keep their relationships with their administrative assistants at arm's length because of these very things. However, there are advantages to creating an open, honest, and friendly relationship with your assistants. The new principal needs friends and insight into the new territory, and there is no better place to start than with the administrative assistant, a person who might just be able to run the school quite well on her own.

SO MANY NEW FRIENDS

The first six months serving as a principal in a new school can be invigorating or exhausting. It's invigorating to finally have the administrative appointment you've dreamed of. It's invigorating to be recognized, celebrated, and even kowtowed to just a little bit. If you're an extrovert, being the new principal means that a whole new universe of people wants to be in your orbit, which is what an extrovert thrives on. The new principal gets interviewed and photographed, and her opinion is sought on all kinds of matters.

However, if that new principal is an introvert, then those first six months are utterly exhausting. Introverts recharge by being alone or in small-group settings, and it is difficult to do that in the first six months. The new principal of a high school meets hundreds of people, has to learn so many names, and has to be open and welcoming to all. That's tiring. The introverted principal needs to develop her own systems for figuring out how to get through that challenging time. Regardless of the new principal's personality, it's important that she figure out her routines for releasing stress and recovering her energy during those first six months.

It is also inevitable that during that first summer the new principal will meet with staff who have an agenda they want the principal to support. You don't have to go looking for them. (Trust me, they'll find you.)

YOU GO TO WAR WITH THE STAFF YOU HAVE

Early on in the United States' war in Iraq, Secretary of Defense Donald Rumsfeld was confronted about our military readiness to fight and prevail, and he said something quite remarkable: "As you know, you go to

> ### IN MY EXPERIENCE
> ### A Teacher Asks for a Change
>
> At my first school, one teacher came in to meet with me during my second week to request that she get "her" Honors English classes back in the coming year. She couldn't have been kinder or more deferential to me. She asked lots of questions and seemed genuinely interested in me, my background, everything. But what she really wanted was to teach kids who met her standard as honor students and to leave the teaching of other kids to less senior members of the faculty.
>
> I knew enough from my previous experience that I didn't need to make a decision (everyone was breathing and no one was bleeding), so I told our senior teacher that I'd have to learn more about this and that it would take me some time to look into it. We ended our meeting cordially. And that's when Jamie, my new best friend, came in and gave me a quick thumbnail sketch of why the prior principal had changed the teacher's assignment.
>
> Families of honor students had complained for years, it turned out, and the teacher had been unwilling to change some practices in her honors classes that were simply inappropriate. It had gotten to the point where honor students were simply choosing not to participate in Honors English at the grade level in which our teacher taught the course. The returning assistant principals confirmed all of this, and the English department chair was equally clear that reversing the previous principal's move would be bad for the school. A week and a half later I met with our teacher again and told her, in person, that she would be keeping the schedule of classes that had been put together by the prior administration. She ended up thanking me for my time and consideration of her request, and we parted on good terms.
>
> This simple interaction proved to be a more important thing than I had first thought. It turned out that many, many people knew that our senior teacher had visited me and had asked me to overturn my predecessor's decision. They knew I reached out to others and sought information. And they came to know that I was taking a thoughtful, deliberate, and fair approach to this issue. Later in my time at the school I didn't always have to take so much time to make a decision, but at the very start, being open, deliberate, and fair minded helped establish me as a solid choice to lead the school.

war with the army you have, not the army you might want or wish to have at a later time." His words are so relevant to the situation we have in traditional public schools. Sometime during those first few weeks, the new principal will meet with a staff member who will leave shaking her head and wondering just who hired that soul—and why. Guaranteed. Here are a few general examples of individuals, all tenured teachers, you might meet (or who you've already met) while teaching in and administering public schools:

- A social science teacher who gave his students Thursdays off. Four days a week, he conducted lessons; on Thursdays, the kids did whatever they wanted.
- A well-intentioned *high school* math teacher who required his students to write out multiplication tables every week.
- Another math teacher who spent more time on his cell phone and computer managing his house-flipping business than he did teaching math.
- A science teacher who ended up on *60 Minutes* in a sensational story about the murder of her son (a leader in a white supremacist movement) by her 10-year-old grandson—whom she wanted prosecuted.
- A choral music teacher who missed 80 days of work per school year—while managing to perform several nights a week in a cover band.
- A Teacher of the Year who had no credential in her assigned subject, who assigned little homework and graded less of it, and who could be found routinely on a certain bar stool in the community most nights of the week.

This is a difficult part of our reality in public schools. The teacher employment system, which grants permanent status to 25-year-olds, means that just about every school everywhere has a teacher or two who stopped striving before age 30 and just shouldn't be there. But they are there, and they'll probably still be teaching in your school long after you've moved on. Charter school and privatization advocates hate this aspect of the system—but it is the system, nonetheless.

It doesn't take the new principal long to figure out who these teachers are; her administrative assistant already knows. As the new principal, it becomes your challenge to figure out how to work with every staff member you have, even the knuckleheads. Whether you like it or not, your knucklehead will be given responsibility for looking after and educating other people's children. The new principal's challenge is to figure out how to help each and every soul on the staff do their work better than the year before.

CHAPTER 3 KEY POINTS AND STRATEGIES

1. First impressions are crucial for the new principal.
2. The assistant principal is a manager; the principal is a leader. Know the differences.
3. The principal has left the field of education and has entered the field of politics.

4. Publish, complete, and report the findings of an entry plan.
5. Go slow to go fast.
6. Focus on your relationship with your administrative assistant. She can make or break you.
7. The first six months are exhausting. Have a plan to reenergize.
8. You go to war with the staff you have.

Four

The Prioritized Principal

All students and staff of public primary, elementary, junior high, and senior high schools, and community colleges, colleges, and universities have the inalienable right to attend campuses which are safe, secure and peaceful.
—California Constitution

Management is doing things right; leadership is doing the right things.
—Peter Drucker

The new principal soon becomes very, very busy. There are dozens of people to meet, an entire community to get to know and understand, and a school to open, usually within just a few weeks. While the publication and implementation of an entry plan will go a long way toward making this initial work easier, there is still important work to do that is not part of the entry plan.

As the opening of school approaches, it becomes essential for the new principal to establish some priorities that will guide the use of his time during those first few months. The principal who fails to establish and communicate clear priorities often ends up plagued with dozens of things that detract from the priorities he should be focused on. Worse, not having clear priorities will often lead to the new principal becoming overworked and overwhelmed. Wherever the new principal lands, though, there are a number of things that should be top priorities in those first few weeks.

PRIORITY—KNOW YOUR FACILITY

The meat-and-potatoes aspect of being the school principal is often overlooked or undervalued in the literature. Given the choice between focusing on restrooms or instructional strategies, it is not uncommon for principals to work on instruction since there are usually others in the school district whose responsibility it is to make sure the facility is in good shape.

However, the principal is responsible for just one school; that district official ends up responsible for leaks, power outages, and all manner of difficulties across town every day, and getting him to pay attention to your school while others in the district are experiencing crises of their own can be a challenge. It is the principal's job to be an advocate not just for his building, but for his community. And, it turns out, advocating for and fixing up your building can have an impact on student learning.

In a great study done by the Far West Laboratory for Educational Research and Development, David Dwyer (1984) reported that successful principals tended to focus on two avenues of action: climate and instructional organization. One unnamed principal is especially singled out in the article for first finding ways to cheer up the school's decor with improved lighting, paint, and flooring despite having little in the budget to fund these improvements. How did he do it? He made it a priority, and he chose to tap an unused resource: the families in the community, who proved quite willing to come in and do the things that the district couldn't do by itself. Improving the condition of the building laid a foundation for working on weightier matters, like student conduct, curriculum, and instructional practice.

One thing that will inevitably occur as the new principal walks campus with the plant manager will be the development of a list of things that require attention. The new principal frequently enters his position with some good will and, quite possibly, a little bit of money and grace from the Facilities and Operations division. Typically there are two times in a principal's life cycle in a school when he can leverage additional funds for his building: when he is new, and right before an accreditation or validation visit by external evaluators.

Once that punch list is developed, the principal and the plant manager should go through it together and have the custodial team complete everything it possibly can on the list within their current human and financial resources. The rest of the necessary items should form the basis for discussions the principal will have with district officials. It is worth it to advocate for the school like this, even in hard times. The principal should hold on to the list of items from that first-year walk-through, especially those that are unable to be handled in the first year. They can form the basis of ongoing discussions with the Facilities and Operations division of the school district.

Keeping those issues in the minds of those responsible for the campus makes it more likely that the issues will be addressed once funding is available. Failure to keep those items on the mind of the Facilities and Operations division is easily interpreted to mean that the issue has either been mitigated or isn't really important, which means when funds do become available they are less likely to be put toward those original issues.

> ### IN MY EXPERIENCE
> ### Walking the School
>
> I became a new administrator in a school five times in my career, three times as an assistant principal and twice as a principal. In all five settings, one of the very first things I did was to spend a day walking the buildings and the classrooms, clipboard in hand, with the head custodian. Spending time with the head custodian quickly reminds the principal that a school runs on water, power, and communication systems.
>
> When I became the principal at Magnolia High School, I inherited a school building that had been erected in 1961—and in a hurry. By the time I arrived, the galvanized pipes running through and beneath the school were 50 years old. The electrical system had been upgraded after 40 years to accommodate air conditioning and some computers. We had faucets, toilets, and other essential elements of our water system that were original to the school. And they broke with regularity. While it was beyond my budget and my persuasive powers to re-plumb the school, it was not beyond my power or responsibility to be prepared when things broke.
>
> As I walked the campus with Carlos, he pointed out all kinds of details that would prove useful. He pointed out which restrooms seemed to get more graffiti than others. He showed me the areas on campus prone to flooding in strong rains. He showed me what his staff focused on, and he showed me some things that were difficult for his staff to focus on as a result of cutbacks that had occurred before I arrived.
>
> I learned how to ring the school's bells, how to respond to a fire alarm bell, and how to use the school's public address system. I also learned a great deal from Carlos about other elements of the school, some of which were surprising. He and his crew knew which teachers were needy and which ones took care of business and solved problems on their own. They knew who was obviously kind as well as those whose kindness wasn't evident. Carlos and I spent six years together at Magnolia High, and I'm proud of the slow and steady improvements we were able to make to the facility. I never regretted my time spent with him and his crew because it made me better prepared to lead the school in moments of crisis.

PRIORITY—ENSURE STUDENT SAFETY AND HAVE A FUNCTIONING DISCIPLINE SYSTEM

In California, the state constitution guarantees that all children have the right to attend safe, secure, and peaceful schools. The wise new principal is well served by attending to this domain before school opens under his leadership. The community wants its schools to be clean, orderly, and safe. Above all things, parents trust us with their children, and they expect that they will attend safe and orderly schools. The principal unable to deliver these most basic conditions will be quickly replaced.

It can be very tempting for the new principal to leave matters of student misconduct and the school's disciplinary response to the assistant principals on campus. The new principal has likely just completed several years of service as an assistant principal and is often itching to be done with the work surrounding student misconduct, which is tedious, taxing, and emotionally difficult.

To be sure, the principal needs to spend far less time on student misconduct than he did as an assistant principal, but—especially at the start of his tenure as a principal—remaining focused on student misconduct can prove very revealing. Misbehaving students often serve as canaries in the mine, as early warning systems. Wise principals everywhere know that student misconduct in the classroom varies quite remarkably depending on who the teacher is, and patterns of student misconduct, easily searchable these days with the widespread use of Student Information Systems, can be an important part of the new principal's learning during the entry phase.

Unfortunately, even here in California, too many schools are plagued by violence and bullying. Failure to attend to those matters when they arise can be fatal for the career of a new principal. There is nothing worse for a school than to have a reputation as being unsafe or violent. In particular, bullying and cyberbullying have come to the fore as critical issues to which the principal simply must attend.

At the outset, the new principal must make clear to teachers, counselors, and all other staff that student conduct that includes violence, bullying, or intimidation is a high priority issue requiring immediate attention. The principal should instruct his staff that he wants to be aware of all such issues immediately, even if the response to the issue is delegated to others. Why be notified each time? Because these are the issues that will generate telephone calls from the community to the school or to the district office itself, it is essential that the principal be conversant with what has occurred and, more important, what is being done. It can't be stated often enough: nothing derails a new principal more than his school developing a reputation as unsafe.

The other word school administrators always hear alongside *safety* is *order*. The two are different things, but one learns soon enough that establishing and maintaining systems that promote order sets a tone that leads to safety. Schools bring together large numbers of people, sometimes thousands, and procedures for maintaining order as those thousands move about their day are essential. Again, this is the distinctly un-sexy side of school leadership, but one discovers just how essential

IN MY EXPERIENCE
Responding to an Unsafe School

The issues of safety and order took on special significance for me when I became the new principal at La Sierra High School in 2006. During my first meeting with our superintendent, I asked him to tell me about the school, and he startled me by responding, "Robert, La Sierra is a violent place. It's our fault, and you have to fix it."

As I began working my entry plan, it became clear that there were longstanding conflicts among African American and Latino students. Our primary strategy in responding to these issues had been to "hit the kids hard" with suspensions. Unfortunately, the strategy hadn't worked very well, and as we got into the fall, we knew something was brewing. The conflict came one morning during the nutrition break, as about 50 kids faced off in the quad along racial lines, ready to fight. Fortunately, we were ready for it and intervened before anything other than words had been exchanged. I directed that the kids all be moved into a large room.

By the time I got into the room—after having called my superintendent—the kids were seated in opposing camps staring each other down. I sent for markers and butcher paper and announced that we would be spending the morning in the room together, working on our issues. The kids protested a little, but not much. I explained that, as the new guy, I needed them all to educate me, and we were going to do it in an orderly fashion.

I gave each group markers and butcher paper, and I asked them to get together and write down their grievances about the other group. No one had done that before. Then I asked them to appoint a spokesperson who would explain the grievances on the poster. Ninety minutes into the conversation, I knew I was going to have to keep the kids in the room through the lunch hour because they weren't ready yet to return to the quad.

I directed that lunch for 50 be brought in to our room. A few minutes later, milk, pizza, salad, and fruit were brought over by the cafeteria manger, which is when an interesting thing happened. The manager asked for the bill to be paid; I told her to drop the invoice in my office and that I would get it taken care of, but that wasn't good enough. Our district required her to balance her books on a daily basis, which meant that she needed $110 right then. I was stumped and surprised; I thought I was in charge. Clearly, I wasn't in charge of this problem, and the cafeteria manager wasn't leaving without $110. As it happened, I was carrying a good amount of cash that day, so I did the only thing I could do to get us re-focused: I pulled $110 out of my wallet and gave it to the manager—in full view of all the kids.

Paying for lunch out of my own pocket got quite a response, and it demonstrated the depth of my investment in this issue. I don't think these kids were used to being listened to, and they certainly weren't used to a blond white guy with a completely different background buying them all lunch. That $110 turned out to be the very best money I ever spent at work.

(continued)

> *By the early afternoon, all grievances had been aired, and we had worked out some understandings about how everyone was going to conduct themselves at school going forward. During the ensuing four school years, those kids never fought one another again, and the school became a much safer place. That foundation made it possible for us to eventually achieve unprecedented academic success at the school.*

systems for maintaining order are if one takes over a school that is having trouble maintaining it.

In individual classrooms, wise teachers establish clear procedures right at the start of school, thus creating a businesslike tone that contributes to a successful learning environment. The top-selling book of all time on this subject is *The First Days of School: How to Be an Effective Teacher*, written by Harry Wong. Wong's thesis is extraordinarily simple: when kids enter a classroom, they want to know two things: what to do and that the teacher cares.

Generations of teachers who have read Wong or heard him speak apply his simple lessons by focusing on order. They teach routines and procedures until all students in the class understand them and follow them. Since routines and procedures are simple, and all students can learn them, students in a Wong-style classroom all experience success at the beginning of the term, which is a great foundation for learning the academic material that follows.

Just like a teacher during the first days of school, a new principal should take pains at the start of his tenure in a school to learn about the school's existing routines and procedures. How are the morning drop-off and afternoon pick-up handled? Are the fire drills and lockdown procedures up to date? Do all staff know them? Again, these things are not what new principals dream of doing, nor are they the pithy stuff of the interviews that get one hired in as a principal, but these basics are essential and must be handled so that when school starts everyone is prepared to deal with them.

PRIORITY—UNDERSTAND THE SYSTEMS FOR MAINTAINING ORDER

One of the things that is striking about schools everywhere is that very large numbers of kids move through them in an orderly manner multiple times per day. In the elementary environment, kids move to their classes, to and from recess, to and from lunch, to and from assemblies, and to and from school. In secondary schools, we further move students about the

IN MY EXPERIENCE
Restoring Order

When I became the new principal at Magnolia High School, my team and I encountered a different kind of problem related to safety and order. Violence wasn't a problem at Magnolia, but getting kids into class on time was an enormous problem. We had over 100 kids late to school each day. Dozens more were late to classes during each period of the day, and 100 more arrived late to their fifth period class—right after lunch—each day. The epidemic of tardiness was just killing classroom environments all over campus.

The school's plan for dealing with tardiness required every teacher to issue detentions, via the use of individual NCR forms that they had to write out by hand, for each student every time they were late to class after the third tardy. A copy of the detention slip was given to the student, and the remaining two copies went to the office. Once a detention was served, the detention monitor (a rotating cast of faculty members serving their adjunct duty requirement) would indicate service of the detention, and the remaining two copies would be divided, with one going back to the assigning teacher and the other remaining with the administration.

The problem was that the volume of tardies and detention slips quickly overwhelmed the site administration. Hundreds of detentions went unserved—as had been the case for years. Jaded teachers stopped writing detentions and came up with their own stratagems for trying to get kids into class on time. There was no central database that tracked all those detention slips and unserved detentions, and enforcement of our school policy eventually became toothless and somewhat random.

By Thanksgiving it was clear that we had a massive problem—and that we had had the problem for years. I couldn't let it go on any longer. I spent days with my administrative team looking at the system. We came up with a simplified plan for enforcement. The plan required more administrative oversight and time, but it was evident that we had to do it that way, even though it meant less time the assistant principals would spend in classrooms supporting instruction.

We discussed our revised plan for detention oversight (which included no changes in policy, just changes in procedures) with our department leaders, who gave us approval to go ahead with it. The next week, administrators explained the new system to every student in their English class, and we got started. The new plan was by no means perfect, but we soon had order, and we knew each day who had been assigned detention, who was serving detention, and who had missed detention. It was a super simple thing to get done, but it turned out to be our first win at Magnolia, and it laid the foundation for bigger wins later on.

campus up to seven times per day as class periods change. Over time, all schools develop routines and procedures to ensure that all this movement is safe and orderly, and the new principal would be very wise to pay some attention to these plans and routines before school starts.

In secondary schools, most major student misconduct occurs during times of movement or during lunch. A good first thing to plan out is where each of the administrators will be during passing periods and lunch. In addition to deploying the administrators, it's important to deploy additional campus supervisory personnel in an intentional manner to ensure that students are well supervised and that any potential intruders on the campus can be deterred. External intruders are a serious problem in schools—a bigger problem than kids wishing to leave school. Remember that first walk-through with the plant manager? That walk-through also should include a walk of the school's perimeter, paying particular attention to issues and challenges that may be lurking.

The most valuable resource in all the preplanning about student movement across school campuses is the faculty. Teachers possess enormous power, influence, and knowledge of the students. In elementary schools, they tend to have very specific assignments to manage and monitor students during passing times. Unfortunately, teachers in secondary schools are often much less involved or deployed to manage and monitor student movement. It's important for the new principal to learn in advance what practices are in place regarding the faculty when it comes to passing periods.

Just because teachers in your prior school all stood at the door during passing periods and greeted kids does not mean that you can expect that same practice to be in place at your new school. The wise new principal should begin by learning about what the school's practice already is. Even if it's a practice you may not completely approve of, it may be that things are just fine, orderly, and safe. But watch for it; pay attention to it as school opens. Remember, safety and order are always first priorities.

On the topic of safety and order, make sure you understand how the school handles fire drills and earthquake drills. There will already be plans in place for these, but it's important to review them in advance with your assistant principals. They should be distributed and reviewed with all staff as a matter of course at the opening staff meeting. It's an excellent idea to conduct a fire drill with full evacuation during the first few days of school just to ensure that everyone knows what to do and that the kids are reasonably prepared should there ever be a real need for an evacuation. And finally, it's critical that the new principal review and understand the school's protocol for a lockdown in the event of a threat to safety. (At Magnolia High School, the lockdown protocol was actually posted in every classroom.)

Besides the systems for maintaining physical order in a school, the new principal needs to learn about the school's digital infrastructure, the school's communication and information systems that underlie its operation. Today's schools all feature a Student Information System (SIS) backbone that is used for recording everything from attendance to grades to disciplinary referrals to immunizations.

Besides the SIS, everyone will have an e-mail address. There will be some sort of data system for managing the Individual Education Plans of the students with disabilities. The school will have a website, and the school will very likely have some sort of school-to-home communication platform that can be used to send out e-mails and voice messages to all families. The school will very likely have an assessment system that enables teachers to craft assessments, score them, and catalog and analyze the results of those assessments by class, by grade, and by nearly any other demographic feature one can imagine.

And finally, most schools these days will have some sort of virtual classroom information system that will permit teachers to create, administer, and collect assignments; post supplementary materials; and enable families to track their student's academic progress. In a secondary school, the student body raises money, so there will be a separate accounting system to manage that. Besides all the foregoing systems, the new principal will have to become immersed in the district's budgeting system, usually for the very first time in his career.

It will take the new principal quite a bit of time to become proficient in all elements of the school's digital infrastructure, so it behooves him to make wise choices in his learning. The very first systems the principal should focus on learning are the Student Information System (SIS) and the mass communication system. The SIS enables to principal to look at critical student information: attendance, grades, and conduct. These pieces of information will be most frequently discussed with families in the principal's office.

The new principal needs to become proficient at extracting these basic elements from the SIS right away, because those kinds of issues will come up quickly. He should also learn how to use the mass communication system before school starts. It's important to be able to deliver an e-mail or a recorded message to families in the event of an emergency.

The rest of the various systems are less of a priority for a new principal. You can burn a lot of time studying assessment data, looking at class websites, and studying IEPs. It's not that the principal shouldn't be able to access and use these systems; it may not be a good idea to focus on becoming facile in all the systems right away because all that time spent learning them detracts from the principal's primary job of leading the school. The principal with a passion for data analysis of interim assessments will have plenty of time to learn how to do that in a new school; he'll never have a second chance to ensure that school opens in a safe, orderly, purposeful manner. If school doesn't open that way, nothing else matters.

PRIORITY—MANAGE YOUR TIME

Perhaps the most valuable thing a principal has is his time, so it's important to organize it well in order to make optimal use of it. Most principals give 60 hours a week to their work Monday through Friday, which is as reasonable as can be expected, especially at the beginning of serving a new school. There are several keys to managing the work and oneself effectively so that those 60 hours a week are as effective as possible.

Manage Yourself and Your Team by Objectives

Every school has goals and objectives that find their way into an annual plan. In California, these plans are extensive and are mandated by the state legislature. The principal should share the annual plan with the entire staff of the school. The plan should be shared in detail with the management team, which includes the assistant principals, activities and athletic directors, and the head counselor in a secondary school. In turn, each assistant principal should write their own plan in which they indicate to the principal which goals they will be more focused on. The principal should complete assistant principal evaluations based partly on their effectiveness in achieving the goals and objectives they set for themselves. This simple step is the beginning of the principal delegating and conferring responsibility to his teammates.

Having a solid school plan provides the principal with something important: the option to say no. If something emerges during the school year that is inconsistent with the school plan, the principal has permission to spend very little time on it. This intentional indifference could annoy people at first, but it is more important to keep focused on consistent targets. If the principal lets everything be a target, the job will quickly grow beyond 60 hours a week.

Make Assistant Principals Leaders

Every assistant principal is preparing for the principalship, so the principal should give them important responsibilities. Each assistant principal can lead a task force or committee to work on a significant school issue. Leading a task force or committee requires each assistant principal to do what the principal does: recruit people, understand all points of view, organize the work, and evaluate the effectiveness of the work. It is wise to encourage entrepreneurship among the assistant principals, and their energy, creativity, and connections with the staff can frequently have a big multiplier effect in improving the school.

Get Rid of the Paper

Do away with paper wherever possible. In general, if a piece of paper comes into the principal's office, it should be brought in by the principal's assistant and should most likely leave when your daily meeting is over, perhaps with a post-it note of instructions affixed. Make your assistant the mistress of all files, and make it your practice to stay out of the files as much as possible. The principal very seldom ever needs anything that goes into the files anyway.

Each piece of paper that the principal needs to keep is best stored in binders. Principals like binders because they are portable, and the work of the principal frequently happens outside of the office. Principals should keep separate binders for management team meetings, the budget, the Professional Development Committee, evaluations, the PTA, and data. So when you attend a PTA meeting, just pull that nice, big PTA binder off the shelf and carry it into the meeting—which also sends a message about the importance of the PTA.

Use Technology to Your Benefit

Principals need order, and most like the order that computer technology provides. It's important to develop an orderly electronic filing system for documents, charts, tables, and spreadsheets. The principal's electronic savior, however, is Outlook (or Google Suite)—and your assistant, once again. Make sure that administrator calendars are already set up so that they can be electronically seen and modified by the administrative assistants. Over time, nearly everything in the principal's calendar will be placed there by an assistant. The calendar is also an excellent tool for carving out time for project work or for visiting classrooms. The wise principal blocks out time in his calendar for those functions. If he doesn't, it's too easy to get trapped in the office.

Managing e-mail well saves time and improves effectiveness. The principal should set up separate e-mail folders and rules that automatically move messages from certain senders into specific folders. The principal must read every e-mail received, but he can improve his efficiency by using the system to pre-sort them, just as he will use his assistant to presort snail mail.

On a normal school day, the principal will receive upward of 100 e-mails, so efficiency matters. The superintendent's office should get its own folder. There should be a folder where e-mails from district-wide administrators land. Establish a folder for e-mails from the site management team. Most important, the principal should maintain a folder labeled "Awaiting Action." When you read an e-mail that you know you have to come back to and work on later, move that e-mail into the "Awaiting Action" folder and mark it as unread. Each time you come back to e-mail, you'll see that little visible reminder telling you how many messages are sitting in the "Awaiting Action" folder. This will improve consistency in following up on many matters.

Schedule Regular Meetings

If you ever work in a school that doesn't schedule regular meetings, you'll learn how valuable it is to schedule and hold regular meetings with the site management team. While some make the case for having fewer meetings, regular meetings of a site management team end up saving the principal and everyone else time. Those meetings also provide a structured time for the management team to make sure everyone is on the same page. Everything in a school goes easier as the staff come to understand that the management team speaks with one voice; holding those regular meetings goes a long way toward ensuring that your team develops one voice.

There is a second kind of meeting that is as essential as that regular management team meeting: lunch. The tightest, most together administrative teams do something really simple: they eat lunch together every day. As many discover, it is very difficult for a principal to have a regularly scheduled lunch, but it is essential and should be a priority. Whether that lunch is before the student lunch, after the student lunch, or in between two student lunches, there should be time for an administrative team to sit down and have lunch together. That lunch break with just the assistant principals turns into really valuable time. It is a great opportunity for mentoring, for throwing around ideas, and for just becoming friends. There may be nothing more important for the new or experienced principal to be focused on than that regular lunch.

PRIORITY—ESTABLISH YOUR COMMUNICATION AND WORK STYLE AND COMMUNICATE IT

Once school starts, the new principal is going to get busy, and it will become important to establish communication routines so that staff know how to get things done. Most work in a school should not require the principal's attention on a day-to-day basis. Let's face reality here: running school is all about getting students into classrooms with the right teachers and the right resources; once that's done, the principal shouldn't have a million things to do every day—right? Right! And for the first few days, that may well be true. But things will happen soon enough that will cause staff to bring things to your attention; that's just natural. In order for the staff to work comfortably with the new principal, it's important that the new principal communicate his preferred pathways of communication as well as his work style.

One of the first things the new principal should do is to be explicit about what media fits within his work style. The principal should make it explicitly clear if he prefers e-mail to voice mail or text messages. For most, e-mail makes things clearer, has the bonus of already being in writing, and is easy to forward along with instructions. Voice messages can be frustrating for the principal because there may be little he can do with them in an efficient manner. You have to listen to them, take notes, and then figure out what to do next. Some principals have their assistant review their voice messages, but the principal will still end up having to listen to quite a few of them himself, take notes, and then generate e-mail. It can be inefficient.

During a good day at work, the principal will spend several hours in and out of classrooms, and it is this walking around time that often leads to something new needing to be done. The new principal should have a plan for what he'll do when a staff member's idea or request is presented. The three most common words principals hear each day while walking campus are, "Got a minute?" Unless he is on the way to an emergency situation, the principal needs to have minutes when staff members or students can stop him. Always. That's what they're there for.

When you walk campus, carry a pen and an index card. When someone hits you with a "Got a minute?" the most important thing you can do is to stop and listen. Frequently, that is all that is ever really needed, to be present and to listen. But sometimes those "Got a minute?" moments turn into something that requires deeper attention than just being in a conversation, and that's when the principal should *always* ask for an e-mail from the staff member.

Asking for that e-mail from the staff member (or student) makes it easier to get work done. First, the e-mail will have the effect of making the request more concise. The e-mail format makes it easy to forward the work along, if that is necessary, and the proper use of e-mail folders helps you ensure that you follow up on the request. Not everyone will like the e-mail style of doing business, but they will get used to it, and they will come to see that the principal gets things done because he really does follow up on his e-mail.

The final element of the principal's work style that ought to be considered is time of day. It's a good idea to make it known if you're a morning person, or if you are not a morning person. We all have better times of day to take on problems and to deal with our jobs. For a principal, it's good to be a morning person, though not essential. Arriving early to school creates time to catch up on e-mail. Another benefit of getting an early start is that the staff can have direct, walk-in access to you before school begins. During the school day, the principal is usually not in the office; preferably, he is out on campus in classrooms. The morning is a good time to hear about an issue and to get things done.

The other piece of the principal's schedule that is important to maintain is off hours. You should not do work while at home in the evening. Once you leave school, you should be done. Don't read e-mail at night. Your staff will learn over time that evening is not a good time to call you and, perhaps more important, that you will never call them after you have left the building. You have to establish boundaries or else the time spent on the job will keep growing and growing. Being clear about these things will help you do your work better and will set some boundaries between work and your family.

PRIORITY—BE THOUGHTFUL ABOUT FIRST DECISIONS AND INITIATIVES

Once school gets going and routines begin to get established, soon enough something will emerge that may require the principal to take action. Once that first thing emerges, the new principal will do well to take action slowly and with an abundance of caution. Schools seldom make changes quickly for reasons we have already established: the staff tend to stay in the school for long periods of time, and they wield a surprising amount of power, while the administrators come and go every few years.

The new principal who desires to change a basic routine in order to improve efficiency would be wise to go slowly—very slowly. For a long time, the standard wisdom for new principals was to conduct the first school year without making *any* changes. The new principal can move a little faster than that conventional wisdom has suggested, but only if he has worked a solid entry plan; done a deep dive to understand his new school, its history, and its traditions; and has shared his learning with the staff and community.

Obviously the most important elements of a school's success are its safety, its learning environment, and student academic achievement. The optimal area where a new principal can take some early action is in the area of the learning environment. If he can get some facilities improve-

IN MY EXPERIENCE
Changing an Ingrained Culture of Tardiness

At Magnolia, once we figured out how to assign and track detentions, it became clear within weeks that we needed to work on the underlying problem behind all those detentions: student tardiness to class. Nearly every staff member I spoke to was upset about kids being late to class and the failure of our systems to improve student timeliness. Since there was no central database we could use to deal with tardies, a kid who evenly distributed tardies across all six periods could be late to class 18 separate times before he even had to serve so much as one detention. And since we wiped the tardy slate clean at the beginning of the semester, that same kid could get 18 more tardies without consequence in the second semester.

During our monthly Leadership Team meetings, department leaders reiterated their frustration with this. These were my teacher-leaders, my best teachers, my veteran teachers. Something had to be done. One of my assistant principals wanted to take this on because he had some experience with a system called Start on Time (Safe and Civil Schools, 2016), which he had seen implemented at his previous school. Even if Start on Time wasn't going to be our answer, and I had my doubts, we needed to start somewhere, so my assistant principal and a band of faculty from a variety of departments across the campus were deputized as a task force and were put to work.

I liked the idea of a faculty task force taking ownership of a problem. I was also mindful that John Hattie's research had demonstrated surprisingly positive academic benefits for interventions that improved classroom management and group cohesion, and decreased disruptive behavior (Hattie, 2009, p. 102).

After 90 days of work, our Tardy Task Force reported back to our faculty on what they had learned, and they proposed that we adopt the Start on Time system for the upcoming fall. The system, which would be a major change for Magnolia, featured the following elements:

1. Every teacher was expected to be at their classroom door to greet students during the passing period.
2. Teachers on a conference period were assigned to specific zones of the campus and were directed to encourage kids to get to class on time and to "sweep" those who were late, taking them to the designated office.
3. Swept students were taken to a designated office where a new computer system quickly scanned the barcode on the student's ID card, noted that the student was late, reported how many total tardies for the semester the student had accumulated, and printed a quick check-out ticket that also assigned the student detention for every tardy after the fourth one in a semester. Data from that tardy database automatically uploaded to the school's Student Information System and recorded that the student was tardy.

(continued)

4. Once students were processed, the teachers who swept them walked them to their class.
5. Classroom teachers stopped having to write detentions, and they stopped recording tardies at all, only noting students in their attendance system who were absent. Teachers who took roll early in the period and marked students absent who later turned out to be tardy did not have to make corrections; the database was set up to mark those absent students as tardy.

Because teachers would have to work during the first 5–10 minutes of their conference period, the faculty had to vote to waive a portion of their contract—which they did.

When school began next fall, we were ready to go. We explained the new system to students in their English classes during the first week of school, and at the beginning of week two we implemented the system. The results were immediately extraordinary. Within days, we eliminated all tardiness to class in periods two through six. Kids were surprised to discover that their fourth total tardy meant that they had a detention assignment since the prior system treated all classes separately. Because our teachers were at their doors and in the hallways, misconduct during passing periods vanished just about entirely.

Soon, we saw something we never dreamed we would see: kids actually hurrying, sometimes at a dead run, to get into class on time. Not only did tardiness go way down, overall attendance improved as well, with Average Daily Attendance (which is how schools in California are funded) improving by 2 percent. Our implementation of Start on Time ended up doing something rare: bringing an entire faculty together to operate a system that was clear and simple. Within a year, we began to host visitors who came to see what we had done to make such a dramatic change.

The implementation of Start on Time at Magnolia was not my first choice about where we should focus our energy to improve the school. We still had significant instructional challenges, and many of our teachers were working in very isolated environments with little collaboration. But Start on Time proved to be the right place to start, because it was what the faculty was ready to do. It had the added benefit of getting teachers out of their classrooms every day and teaming with the other teachers in their conference period on sweep duty. For the first time in a long time, a staff-driven intervention unified the staff and measurably improved outcomes all across the campus. It proved to be a perfect first change.

ments, that's terrific. For many, it can be frustrating to focus on something so prosaic as the building or the campus, but you'd be surprised at the positive response from a community whose buildings and grounds are safer, cleaner, more comfortable, and more orderly.

There's often a Hawthorne effect that goes along with those improvements. However, most newer principals aren't hoping to make a mark through these workaday interventions; rather, newer principals are more and more focused on instructional practice—which makes sense in the post–No Child Left Behind era. Even so, there's only so much the new principal can do in the instructional arena with much effect in the first year, particularly if he leads a large school.

For the first year, nearly all principals are best served by ensuring safety and order, working a complete entry plan, and building positive relationships with staff, students, and community. There will already be a school plan in place, and the principal is wise to stick to working on that plan with the school staff. Unified action, even if it may not implement the very best strategy, is nonetheless a powerful force.

Within the first few months, if there are problems or challenges in the school not being addressed by implementing the existing school plan, they will emerge. And that's when the new principal may very well have to take action. This, of course, violates the adage of making no changes during the first year, but many a principal has managed to safely navigate some change during the first year.

The key to a substantive change or initiative during the first year is to delegate the study of the problem to the staff. After all, they know more about it than the principal, and it's possible they've been discussing this issue for some time. Establishing a task force to address an ongoing issue also provides an assistant principal with a great leadership opportunity if the issue is such that the principal does not have to be present at all the meetings.

CHAPTER 4 KEY POINTS AND STRATEGIES

1. It's critical that the new principal knows his facility well.
2. A school runs on water, power, and communication systems.
3. Always be mindful of the first directive: when in doubt, attend to safety, security, and order.
4. Learn your school's digital infrastructure. Master the Student Information System first.
5. Time is the coin of your realm. Manage it!
6. Eliminate paper wherever you can.
7. Establish and publicize your preferred communication style.

8. Be clear and thoughtful about the time limits of your work and availability. It's okay to set some limits.
9. It's a good idea to keep your big decisions and initiatives focused on safety, order, and the facilities.
10. The first initiative you undertake will be critical. It needs staff buy-in, and it needs to be successful. Remember: win small, win early, win often.

Five

The Strategic Principal

Never doubt that a small group of thoughtful, committed people can change the world. Indeed, it is the only thing that ever has.—Margaret Mead

A school can fulfill no higher purpose than to teach all its members that they can make what they believe in happen.—Roland Barth

If you want to go fast, go alone. If you want to go far, go together.
—African Proverb

Once school has settled and is running, safety and order is attended to, and the entry plan work is nearing completion, the new principal reaches a point where she will find herself looking for answers to a compelling question: What will be her strategy to improve student academic achievement in her school? How the principal contemplates this question and ultimately responds to it will go a long way toward determining if she is a successful principal. The wise principal in a new school takes a thoughtful, measured approach to the development and implementation of a strategy to improve academic achievement.

WHAT WAS LEARNED FROM THE ENTRY PLAN?

Schools are very seldom blank slates, since nearly every school that selects a principal is not brand new. That the school is not new is an important element sometimes overlooked by principals with more hubris than sense. One occasionally runs into a case where a new principal, full of confidence that reciprocal teaching, project-based learning, microteaching, whole language, AVID strategies, or thinking maps (insert your preferred intervention here) simply must be implemented right away and proceeds to do her best to ramrod this new program throughout a campus. Some principals can pull it off, but most encounter faculty resistance and fail to capitalize on the single most powerful force in the building: the power of a unified faculty.

More than a few new principals, driven by ambition, hubris, or a sincere belief in an intervention that worked for them in a previous setting, have inadvertently come to learn about the power of a unified faculty once that power is turned against them by teachers angry at having a new program forcefully implemented across a campus. We have a name for those principals—one and done—because they tend to last for about one year in their assignment. No one should ever have to be a one and done principal if she does what is smart: patiently work through an entry plan while remaining focused at the outset on safety, order, and the overall learning environment.

This is where the wise principal should return to her entry plan and take some time to analyze all the information she has collected from interviews, meetings, program reviews, accreditation self-study documents, the annual school plans, and student achievement data. Those first six months working through the entry plan process will push the principal to do a lot of work because there is simply so much out there to review. People who criticize schools for not being focused enough on results have no idea just how focused on student achievement data they really are.

In fact, they're drowning in data. The level of detailed data to which a principal has access is quite startling. Just about any principal could easily report out how well Latino boys with IEPs demonstrate attainment of specific science standards on classroom assessments—and she could even determine which teacher's Latino boys with IEPs were doing better.

By the time the new principal gets to winter break, it's time to stop and take a breath and begin to summarize the most important things she has learned about her school and to prepare to report them out to the school, the district, and the community. It is helpful to organize her analysis and report in this manner:

1. A description of the process
2. Findings from interviews
   a. Strengths
   b. Issues and concerns
   c. Suggested priorities (from interviewees)
3. A summary of student academic achievement
4. How things have gotten done around here
5. We should continue to . . .
6. We need to start . . .
7. Some potential new directions

Organizing the findings of the entry plan in this manner does several things for the new principal. First, it gives her a chance to demonstrate that she has worked hard to learn about where she is. She'll find it very difficult to bring together a staff she hasn't learned much about.

Second, the first things that are reported are those things learned from the interviews. This values the input of the staff and really should serve as the starting point for developing a strategy. It's not unusual for the new principal to determine her strategy for improving the school just through the interviews. Teachers are smart; they usually know what needs to be done to improve student achievement, and it would behoove the new principal to pay close attention to the suggestions that emerge from those interviews.

It's also important for the new principal to take the time to learn about how new programs and interventions have come to pass at the school prior to her being there, which is why one heading for the entry plan report is about how things get done at the school. She may learn that the very best work on her campus arose from a group of committed teachers. She may learn that her new school has a history of just waiting to be told by the district what they should work on next. Or, she may learn that she's in a school that has stuck like glue to the tenets of its founding vision. Regardless of what she learns, it's critical for the principal to understand how changes have succeeded and failed at her school if she is planning to implement a new strategy.

By the time a new principal goes home for her well-deserved winter break and to begin her analysis of the information gathered during the entry plan, she probably already has a strategy germinating in her mind. This should be expected of someone who has served as a teacher and co-administrator with excellence and has made it through the rigors of the principal selection process. Let's remember: these positions are extremely difficult to get, and the 21st-century principal is expected to be a transformational leader, not a mere manager. However, before she spends her winter break developing that strategy, our new principal would be wise to do a little more learning before proceeding.

WHAT IS YOUR DISTRICT DOING?

An important element of the entry plan process is all that learning about what the district has been doing to support the school in its work to improve student academic achievement. The new principal can learn a great deal in her discussions with the superintendent, assistant superintendents, and directors. If the principal is in a new district, then it is vital to understand what the district's strategy has been to improve student achievement. A principal should realize that what the district has previously focused on will have clear impact on what she is able to do strategically.

A second element of district support for implementing an improvement strategy is funding. Our new principal needs to have a clear awareness of just what funding commitment her district can make toward implementing whatever improvement strategy emerges. Most school improvement efforts cost more money than is generally allocated in the budget, so it is important for the principal to have learned during the entry planning process just what resources will be available to her as her school implements a strategy to improve student achievement.

WHAT WOULD THE EXPERTS HAVE YOU DO?

When a new principal spends that first winter break contemplating her strategy to improve student academic achievement in her school, it's also an excellent time to review what the experts and more prominent thinkers about school leadership have learned about how to improve schools. In this day and age, a principal who intends to implement a strategy to improve student achievement in her school must always answer a key first question: What do the experts say about your strategy? This is a legitimate question, particularly when you realize that a strategy to improve a school will have a direct impact on other people's children.

If there isn't a solid theory or research base that supports a proposed direction, very few school districts will permit a principal to move forward with her strategy; it would be irresponsible. While it is beyond the scope of this book to provide an exhaustive discussion of the state of the research on effective strategies for school improvement, there are a number of prominent practitioners and researchers whose work provides a firm foundation on which to base a school improvement strategy.

Roland Barth

Even though he's not really a researcher, Roland Barth is a great starting point for any principal to turn to when seeking a strategy to improve a school. Barth was a teacher, a principal, and the founding director of the Harvard Principals' Center. Thousands of principals have been fortunate to learn directly from Barth at Harvard, at symposia across the country, and through reading his published work. Barth brings a sense of wisdom, perspective, and focus to his work, which centers on some core practices: a focus on the relationships among the adults in a school, the idea of the principal as lead learner, the value of the principal regularly writing to the staff, and encouraging teachers to step out and try new things—to take risks. Barth describes his beliefs and his vision for a good school most comprehensively in *Improving Schools from Within* (1990). The key elements of Barth's vision of a good school are the following:

- The school as a community of learners
- A place characterized by high levels of collegiality among the faculty
- A place where risk-taking is honored and supported
- A place where every adult recommits to being and working at the school by their own choice and commitment
- A place where there is respect for diversity
- A place for philosophers
- A place characterized by humor
- A place led by a community of teacher-leaders
- A place characterized by low anxiety and high standards (Barth, 1990)

Who wouldn't want to lead a school like this one? It's a compelling vision, and a new principal would be wise to study the facets of Barth's vision and compare them to where her school is presently in its growth and development. Of course, envisioning such a school is not nearly as difficult as the day-to-day work our new principal must do if she is to transform her school into something like the one Barth describes.

Kenneth Leithwood and the Wallace Foundation

Kenneth Leithwood is a distinguished researcher at the University of Toronto who was the lead author on the Wallace Foundation's 2004 report on how leadership influences student learning. That study found that there are three basic leadership practices that influence student learning:

1. setting directions;
2. developing people; and
3. redesigning the organization (Leithwood et al., 2004, p. 8).

Setting directions accounted for the greatest impact on student achievement. Actions that were a part of setting directions included identifying and articulating a vision, fostering the acceptance of group goals, and creating high performance expectations. Monitoring organizational performance and promoting effective communication throughout the organization also help develop shared organizational purpose. Developing people means exactly what it says: implementing practices that cause teachers to engage in deeper professional learning.

That third element—redesigning the organization—doesn't necessarily mean exactly what it says. What the authors were describing here is implementing practices that enabled teachers to flourish in their work and to grow as educators. Practices that fell under this orbit included strengthening school culture, building collaborative processes, and modifying structures if they were preventing the use of effective educational practices.

Much like Barth, Leithwood found that the most important work a principal should do is to focus on supporting and developing skilled, collaborative teachers. In a subsequent publication in 2007, Leithwood and his collaborators report the results of a large-scale study in Canada on developing distributed leadership, continuing the theme that teacher empowerment and leadership are keys to improving student learning.

Michael Fullan

Another expert to whom our new principal should turn is Michael Fullan, now professor emeritus at the University of Toronto. Fullan devoted his career to studying transformational leadership in schools and then trying to work with large-scale educational systems to improve the implementation of change. In *The Principal: Three Keys to Maximizing Impact* (2014), he acknowledges the enormity of our challenge in serving as the principal and offers three areas where the principal should focus her energies:

1. leading learning,
2. being a district and system player, and
3. becoming a change agent.

Fullan has long focused on what he calls change drivers, which he divides into two kinds: right drivers and wrong drivers. The wrong drivers of change are:

1. Accountability
2. Individualistic solutions
3. Technology
4. Fragmented strategies

The right drivers of change are:

1. Capacity building
2. Collaborative effort
3. Pedagogy
4. Systemness

By individualistic solutions, Fullan is referring to the notion that a school's problems can be traced to certain individuals and that replacing those individuals will solve the problems. While this idea has an allure to every principal who has encountered a whiny, burned-out teacher, Fullan dismisses it as unworkable and ineffective, arguing that the best way to deal with individuals not doing their best is to use the power of a group of teachers to change a group of teachers. Like Barth and Leithwood, Fullan would have our new principal remain squarely focused on building the capacity of her faculty and by working on improving the collaborative culture. In one of the key sentences in his book, Fullan provides our principal with a great piece of advice:

> In all of the literature about principals who lead successful schools, one factor comes up again and again: *relational trust*. When it comes to growth, relational trust pertains to feelings that the culture supports continuous learning rather than early judgements about how weak or strong you might be. (Fullan, 2014, p. 75)

Fullan's decades of research and consultation with school systems in Canada and the United States lends further power and authority to what Barth first described in 1990: the best schools operate as communities of learners.

New Leaders

New Leaders was originally developed in 2000 as New Leaders for New Schools, an organization that began as a proposal by a group of graduate students at Harvard. The gist of their proposal was to develop and scale up a training program for candidates to serve as principals in charter schools and in underserved urban areas. The proposal won the Business Plan completion at the Harvard School of Business, and its founders subsequently were successful in attaining start-up funding, most notably from the Bill and Melinda Gates Foundation and the Boeing Company.

New Leaders stands alone as a multi-state training ground for principals, now with over 15 years of experience training principals, and they have recently published *Breakthrough Principals: A Step-by-Step Guide to Building Stronger Schools* (Desravines, Aquino, and Fenton, 2016), a substantial book that outlines their approach to school leadership and contains detailed instructions and support for the principal intending to lead a school in a manner consistent with New Leaders' approach. Whether you like the idea of a national training ground for principals or not, New Leaders is a powerful force and voice in school leadership. Over the course of those 15 years, New Leaders has developed a model for school leadership that divides school leadership into five broad areas:

1. Learning and teaching
2. School culture
3. Talent management
4. Planning and operations
5. Personal leadership

Within each of the five broad areas, New Leaders has identified key levers the principal can employ if improvement in the area is needed. It is the new principal's responsibility to review each of the five areas, identify principal actions and school actions that might be of use, and then implement those actions. Each of the levers is described in some detail within the text, and the book concludes with a principal's tool kit, which includes over 50 pages of assessment tools, reflective questions, and templates for organizing one's work. No other book has put together such a comprehensive guide to school improvement from the principal's office. A principal in search of strategies for improving her school will find plenty of concrete suggestions from New Leaders.

One Simple Chart

It is often useful to summarize ideas in simple charts and tables. To that end, table 5.1 is a very simple summary of the big ideas from Barth, Leithwood, Fullan, and New Leaders.

This chart demonstrates that the new principal contemplating a strategy for school improvement can approach her school through a number of lenses, depending on what she has learned during her entry plan work. Part of the art of leadership will be to determine through which lens it is best to assess the school's present reality.

DON'T ROW ALONE

Principals often wish they had more autonomy and authority as a school principal so that they and their staff could just get to work on improvement strategies. Most principals feel this way at some point. It is easy to bemoan the districts' various initiatives, the misguided (to principals) priorities of school boards, and the constant creep of district programs into what used to be the principal's sphere of autonomy.

A new principal will definitely be contemplating this as she tries to pull together a strategy for improving student achievement in her

Table 5.1. Summary: The Big Ideas in School Leadership

Roland Barth	Kenneth Leithwood	Michael Fullan	New Leaders
• the school as a *community of learners* • high levels of *collegiality* among the faculty • a place where *risk-taking* is honored and supported • a place led by a community of *teacher-leaders* • a place characterized by *low anxiety and high standards*	**Three Leadership Practices:** 1. setting directions 2. developing people 3. redesigning the organization **Key Practices:** • supporting and developing skilled, collaborative teachers • implementing distributed leadership	**Three Keys to Maximizing Impact:** 1. leading learning 2. being a district and system player 3. becoming a change agent **Right Change Drivers:** • capacity building • collaborative effort • pedagogy • systemness **Wrong Drivers:** • accountability • individualistic solutions • technology • fragmented strategies	**Five Categories:** 1. learning and teaching 2. school culture 3. talent management 4. planning and operations 5. personal leadership **Process:** • conduct an assessment in all five areas • identify and implement appropriate levers within the categories to improve

school. She will struggle with the challenge of how to unify the faculty behind her strategy, to be sure. But before she begins that work, she has a much more important player whose participation and support she must enlist: her district administration and, possibly, the school board who appointed her.

Comprehensive public schools are massive enterprises, often housed on prime land, featuring expensive buildings; they are a source of pride in most communities. Schools are also intensely politicized these days, with their curriculum and methods endlessly debated and frequently excoriated by people who know little about what helps kids learn.

Whether we like it or not, K–12 education is an immense industry, funded with public money. In California, voters have approved Proposition 98, which ensures that no less than 40 percent of our state's entire budget is to be spent annually on schools. That sounds like a lot of money—until one realizes that per student funding in California ranks 27th in the country (National Education Association, 2015, p. 55). Against this background, it's easy to see why a new principal isn't likely going to be left to her own devices to implement her preferred strategy.

Whether she likes it or not, she's going to have to gain support from her district before implementing a new strategy. And once that strategy is implemented, she's most likely going to end up accountable for its results. That's the nature of schools. The days of the lone wolf principal fearlessly and heroically reforming a school on her own disappeared long ago, at about the exact same time that school districts became accountable for student learning as measured and reported on statewide tests.

The new principal will not be rowing her boat alone; she will be part of a larger crew—which turns out to be a good thing. The rowing metaphor works as a starting place for envisioning school improvement. I was a collegiate rower in eight-oared boats, and I rediscovered the sport in my 50s. I am now an enthusiastic rower of a single several times each week. Getting a single out of the boathouse and into the water goes quickly.

At the same time I put my one-man boat in the water, the women's program at my rowing club launches two eight-oared shells, and it takes a while. There are oars and seating arrangements to coordinate and a meeting with the coach who explains the workout and the day's goals; only then do the ladies get their boat to the water, get in it, and get going. By the time they start, I am out of sight and already well into my workout.

But later on in the workout, that eight-oared shell will just smoke right past me, moving at a speed simply unattainable in a single. In my delicate single, I am the picture of calm, balance, and technical mastery, while those eight women in their shell are somewhat less skilled, and they even need a passenger in the back to steer for them! And yet, they just race past me. Their coordinated power—even if it lacks the precision of my delicate technical rowing in the single—trumps individual progress every time.

Of course, the same dynamic is true of school improvement: a group of committed, aligned people always accomplish more in school than heroic individual efforts, which is why the new principal needs her district alongside her as she prepares to implement her strategy for improving student achievement. While she might be able to get started faster on her own, she'll never sustain the necessary speed and momentum if she continues to go it alone. The truth of rowing and school improvement is this: even lousy eights always zip past talented singles—once they get in the boat and get going.

USE THE PROCESSES ALREADY IN PLACE

An ongoing theme in this book has been the idea that nearly all schools are not new and that they already have systems and processes in place, often placed there by the school board or even the state legislature. In California, schools have ensconced ongoing improvement systems that are required by state law: the Single Plan for Student Achievement (SPSA), and the Western Association of Schools and Colleges (WASC), the accreditation process for high schools.

A critical part of the new principal's entry plan had her reading her school's prior SPSA and accreditation documents. For the last few years in California, school districts have also had to write and implement Local Control and Accountability Plans (LCAP) in which they spell out how they are using state funds to address eight mandatory state priorities in schools. (Readers in other states will also find that their schools have similar documents but that they will go by different names.) These documents are critical because they are required and ongoing and must be approved by the school board before they are submitted. The other important element of the SPSA and the WASC reports is that they represent the work of the entire school staff. Many hands are involved in the production of this work, and the participatory nature of the documents plays a role in implementing the plans the documents contain.

The new principal who plans to implement a new strategy for improving student achievement needs to get the strategy (and its funding, if necessary) into the school's planning documents. While it's tempting to just start the new strategy, it's important that the strategy and its funding get secured in the school/district plan as soon as possible. Once the strategy is named, funded, staffed (if necessary), and assigned some benchmark data by which to measure its success, it is far more likely that the strategy will become a lasting element of the institution rather than a passing fad.

SUCCESS MEANS MEASURING AND REPORTING PROGRESS

One of the most critical elements of implementing a school improvement strategy is the selection, measurement, and reporting of data about student progress. Student progress is what matters here, not data about meetings held, trainings attended, or the attitudes and satisfaction of the staff. The most important thing to measure is simply this: Are students doing better and learning more as a result of the strategy the school is implementing?

It used to be that we had very little data to look at—if we even looked at all. How quaint. Since the latter 1990s, schools have begun to drown in data, causing many wags to label some schools as places where DRIP (data rich, information poor) seemed to be the prevailing situation. The principal's challenge, along with her site Leadership Team and her district, is to select meaningful data points, report them out to the staff and community at the outset, and then to keep reporting that data out as the strategy is implemented, using intervals that make sense.

The principal must strive to report data that matters to students and to teachers at regular intervals. Without question, the most important data point to students and families in secondary schools are grades reported at quarters and semesters. It's surprising that we don't pay greater attention to course grades, since no other measure matters so much to students, their families, and their teachers.

Principals should make it a practice to report grade distributions by course at the close of each academic quarter. There is a clear benefit to regularly reporting this data: over time, it will improve. Teachers and department leaders know that improving college eligibility and academic achievement for students is a primary focus, and leaders among them will begin to take steps on their own to try to improve student grades. Merely reporting grade distributions will likely cause teachers who used to put zeroes in their grade books for missing assignments to start giving kids second chances. Reporting grade distributions can lead to spirited discussions about whether zero is even a fair mark to record in a system where 59 percent is, technically, an F.

The regular reporting of different kinds of data can have a positive effect on staff morale as well. Faculty want to see their data improve, and they will take all kinds of individual steps to positively impact it. In short, what they attend to is what is likely to improve. In many schools, just reporting the data and making it a feature of Leadership Team discussion a few times a year will likely lead to improvement, even if the principal hasn't yet developed a strategy herself for improving the specific data point. Shining a light on data turns out to be an improvement strategy in itself.

At La Sierra High School, a team of biology teachers became a true Professional Learning Community (PLC) after their continued frustration with student achievement in biology. They were distressed at a high failure rate and relatively low scores on the state's end-of-year biology assessment. Their strategy to improve involved going all-in on the PLC model, mapping key curricular elements and abandoning some old favorites, and aligning their instruction, pacing, and assessments.

At the end of five weeks of instruction, every biology student took a common assessment the team designed to determine if they were proficient. Proficient students spent the next week in enrichment activities, while those not yet proficient spent that next week in an intervention setting where key concepts were re-taught, using a different strategy, which was followed up by an alternate form of the prior week's assessment. The higher score was counted.

Every six weeks, the biology team would share out the proportion of students who needed intervention and those who would participate in the enrichment; by the end of the year, the proportion of students requiring intervention declined dramatically. They became very focused on the data from their interim assessments, and they shared their best strategies with one another. It was electrifying to watch their work. The final proof of the team's success arrived over the summer, when results from the state's end-of-year biology test showed an improvement in the percentage of students proficient in biology from 39 percent to 60 percent in one year, an incredible single-year gain.

Teachers respond to data that matters to them and to their students. No student has ever wanted to fail nor has there been a teacher who wanted to award failing grades. But in the absence of regular data review, people grow complacent. Surprisingly, principals will encounter teachers who really aren't aware of the data about how their students—and by extension, themselves—are doing. When they start to study it (or have it reported back to them by their administration every nine weeks), they will almost always develop motivation to try something new, to see if they can do something what will have a positive impact on results.

UNLEASH THE POWER OF THE STAFF

The Kenyan proverb that says that sticks in a bundle are unbreakable is such an accurate metaphor for school improvement. Whatever the new principal does in her new school, she must implement a strategy that will unify and unleash the power of the staff. A faculty that faithfully implemented reciprocal teaching twice each week would surely produce gains in student achievement. That same faculty would also see improved student achievement if they all implemented a school-wide program to improve classroom cohesion, such as Capturing Kids' Hearts. Gains would surely follow if an entire faculty faithfully implemented metacognitive instructional strategies (Hattie, 2009). Whatever strategy the principal contemplates, her most important work won't be the training and professional development about the strategy; her most important work will be to build a unified faculty who enthusiastically embrace the strategy and will implement it faithfully and enthusiastically.

WHAT BEING SUCCESSFUL REALLY MEANS

This book aims to answer one big question: What does it take to be a successful principal? The International Successful Principals Project was designed to study principals across a variety of countries and to look for common threads in those judged successful. As part of that work, headquartered in England at the University of Nottingham, Christopher Day produced this description of success:

> Success includes, but is more than, effectiveness. . . . In general, we may say that "effectiveness" is associated with instrumental outcomes of students (tests, examination results), whereas success is associated with these in addition to positive personal and social outcomes, well-being, and equity. In other words, success is more all-encompassing. More complex to discern than the sets of bullet points, good advice, and other indicators so readily available from the plethora of school effectiveness research, policy documents, and training and development program documentation. (Day, 2007, p. 15)

The principal who secures a position, successfully navigates the hazards of entry, and is able to lead a school with improving student achievement is clearly effective. Given the high turnover in principals' offices, a principal who is able to achieve the foregoing is justified in being proud of her achievements. Indeed, there are many principals just like her who quickly move on to another school or are promoted into district-level leadership positions. Sometimes their schools continue to grow after their departures; sometimes they stagnate.

The successful principal is more transformational in effect than an effective principal. The effective principal does her job well and usually moves on; the successful principal also does her job well, but in so doing it she transforms the capacity of the school so that it will continue to grow when she departs, regardless of who succeeds her. This continuous upward trajectory occurs as a result of the successful principal's ongoing focus in developing others and her commitment to leadership in her school, usually for a longer period of time. In the chapters that follow, we'll explore what the successful principal can do to avoid traps, build effective teams, and motivate her staff to continuous improvement.

CHAPTER 5 KEY POINTS AND STRATEGIES

1. Report your entry plan findings clearly and publicly, ensuring that you report what was learned from the faculty.
2. Any improvement strategy the new principal is considering must be based on findings from the work of the entry plan.
3. The new principal must be aware of what her district is doing to improve the school before devising a strategy of her own.
4. The new principal should know what the experts have to say about strategies to improve student achievement.
5. Nearly all improvement strategies suggested by experts have this in common: they rely on the power and efficacy of a unified staff.
6. Don't row alone. Eights move faster than singles. Your district is an eight.
7. Study and make use of the improvement processes in place in your setting. Use the school and district plan documents to put an improvement strategy into place.
8. No strategy is successful unless the principal can report data that is clear, unassailable, and linked to the implemented strategy.
9. Always change a losing game; never change a winning game.
10. There are two parts to being a successful principal: (1) improved student achievement results and (2) positive personal and social outcomes, well-being, and equity. The effective principal accomplishes the former, while the successful principal goes beyond those instrumental outcomes.

Six

The Defined Principal

Kids don't remember what you try to teach them. They remember what you are.—Jim Henson

To lead the people, walk behind them.—Lao-Tzu

Be more concerned with your character than your reputation, because your character is what you really are, while your reputation is merely what others think you are.—John Wooden

A school principal is a prominent, studied, and much discussed public servant. While teachers are prominent in the dinner table discussions of a few families, the principal, at times, ends up in the dinner table discussions of hundreds and, occasionally, thousands of people. The brave men and women who leave teaching for school administration—and make no mistake, they *are* brave—trade the autonomy, power, and privacy of the classroom teacher for the privilege of leading an entire school and its community. An inevitable consequence of being the principal is that people form their own impressions of who the principal is, and those impressions will have an impact on how successful the principal proves in his work.

It's no surprise to any of us that contemporary leaders in politics and business devote considerable resources to cultivating their images. Public relations specialists abound, with the United States Department of Labor (2016) reporting that California alone employed 28,820 men and women in those positions in 2015 (recall that the state has about 14,500 school principals) and that nationally 218,910 individuals were working in that occupation. The image of an organization and its leaders matters deeply, and that's why so many business leaders work with public relations specialists to define their image or brand.

In recent years, schools and school districts have worked with public relations consultants to identify and improve their brands as they have faced competition for students from charter schools. A new principal needs to proceed thoughtfully in his work in order to define his image if he intends to be successful. A principal who gets tagged with a bad image is increasingly likely to be removed from his position in these competitive, high-pressure times for schools.

GOING BACK TO ARISTOTLE: THE CONCEPT OF ETHOS

In order to get anything done in his school, the principal must be able to generate support from his faculty. Rarely does the principal command. More often, the principal develops teams, motivates them to work, and persuades them to take on initiatives that will improve student achievement. The principal should be imagined in the context of a persuader, as opposed to a manager. Getting important work done in public schools requires the consent and the active engagement of the school's staff. The principal, purely on the basis of positional power, cannot command a staff to engage in a new strategy with initiative and enthusiasm. And this is where the wisdom of the ancients who developed the study of rhetoric, particularly Aristotle, is worth consulting.

Rhetoric is the study of how speakers and writers use various techniques to create meaning, to persuade. Though the word *rhetoric* these days usually has a bad connotation associated with it (think of political rhetoric), the study of rhetoric was part of the backbone of the classical education afforded ancient Greeks and Romans, particularly those who aspired to political leadership. In the fourth century BCE, Aristotle's *Rhetoric* described the three major means of persuasion as ethos, pathos, and logos (Honeycutt, 2011).

The most highly valued of the three means of persuasion was logos, which refers to the use of logical arguments that stand up to intellectual scrutiny. The most suspect of the means of persuasion was pathos, a word that survives today in regular usage and refers to strategies designed to elicit an emotional response from an audience. We see the use of pathos all the time in contemporary political discourse as speakers and writers routinely invoke fears of impending disaster. Positioned between these two means of persuasion is the idea of ethos, which refers to the character of the speaker. In the rhetorical sense, ethos is about more than just the character of the speaker; it also encompasses the notion that a speaker can construct an ethos through careful selection of diction and argumentative strategies. In the rhetorical sense, everything one says or writes contributes to one's ethos.

It was Aristotle who put in writing the basic ideas of ethos: an audience wants to feel some connection with a speaker. An audience wants to see some aspect of their better selves in a speaker and his ideas. An audience wants to put their trust in a speaker whose experience is somewhat like their own, though perhaps deeper. An audience wants to like a speaker. These things all mean that the successful speaker must share enough through his speech (verbal or written) so that the audience can establish a positive conception of just who it is they are hearing.

When you think about it, this sounds a lot like what those 218,910 public relations professionals do for a living, doesn't it? They strive to define their client or its product in such a way that the audience (or market) is compelled, is persuaded. While a school principal doesn't need to consult a public relations specialist, which would be *disastrous* if ever publicly known, the principal needs to be clear about who he is and how he will go about defining himself to his audiences.

CONCEPTIONS OF ETHOS IN THE BUSINESS WORLD

Business leaders intentionally build ethos, often with substantial impact. When you think of Apple Computer's Steve Jobs, don't you see him in jeans and a black turtleneck? Facebook founder Mark Zuckerberg will forever be envisioned in a T-shirt and hoodie. These men set out to disrupt their industries and take them over, and the audiences they were most concerned with were not impressed by men in dark business suits wearing blue ties. But ethos isn't just created by the manner in which one dresses; it's created by all kinds of choices one makes in one's lifestyle, one's speech, one's writing, and through one's daily work.

The culture of business has always venerated the men and women in executive suites and boardrooms, which was true on a grand scale during the late 1980s and the 1990s when swashbuckling chief executive officers jumped from company to company, doing various kinds of restructuring deals, landing on the covers of news magazines, and writing autobiographies. One of the archetypes of this era was Albert Dunlap, a man who rose to become the CEO of Scott Paper and, later, Sunbeam.

Dunlap came to be known as "Chainsaw Al" during his tenure at Scott Paper, where he cut the workforce of 30,000 by one-third. Dunlap was a turnaround specialist who focused relentlessly on doing whatever it took to return value to shareholders. He had little sympathy for workers and argued that he had little obligation to them. Echoing Harry Truman's words, he let people know that if they wanted to have a friend, they should get a dog, since it was not his job to be anybody's friend. His job was to return value to shareholders.

For two years of work at Scott Paper, which eventually was merged into Kimberly-Clark, Dunlap walked away with $100 million and then published a book titled *Mean Business: How I Save Bad Companies and Make*

Good Companies Great. Talk about establishing an ethos! It's difficult to imagine a principal coming into town with the kind of ethos Al Dunlap brought with him and turning around a school.

At the same time our country saw the emergence of these high-flying CEOs, another leadership movement was developing that took a different direction, and one of its best spokesmen was Robert Greenleaf, who had served as an executive at AT&T before transitioning into service as a lecturer and founder of what ultimately exists today as the Robert K. Greenleaf Center for Servant Leadership. Greenleaf believed that true power as a leader came from the consent of those led, which he described in this way:

> [T]he only authority deserving one's allegiance is that which is freely and knowingly granted by the led to the leader in response to, and in proportion to, the clearly evident servant stature of the leader. (Greenleaf, 1977, p. 10)

Greenleaf saw that the best leaders were focused on the needs of all people in an organization, and he posed a test to ascertain if a leader was doing right:

> The best test, and difficult to administer, is: Do those served grow as persons? Do they, while being served, become healthier, wiser, freer, more autonomous, more likely themselves, to become servants? (Greenleaf, 1977, p. 14)

The ethos of the servant leader is much different than the ethos of the corporate turnaround specialist, and it is a much more appropriate model to follow in school leadership. After all, the goal of the successful principal is to improve student achievement in his school, and that only happens when his teachers come together and do better work—when they grow as teachers and become "healthier, wiser, freer, more autonomous" (Greenleaf, 1977, p. 14). Greenleaf and subsequent writers and thinkers, including Ken Blanchard, Steven Covey, and Peter Senge, changed the conversation about the ethos of the leader.

Jim Collins, author of *Good to Great*, has done the most to define the ethos of the contemporary servant leader. Collins and a team of researchers studied over 1,000 companies for five years and eventually identified 11 that made great sustained growth. As they dug into those 11 companies, Collins's team studied their leaders, and they found that those 11 companies had leaders who were modest. Instead of finding Lee Iacocca, Jack Welch, or Al Dunlap in the executive suite, they found quieter men (yes, men) who were characterized by personal humility and professional will. Collins labeled these men Level 5 Leaders, and he described their unwavering focus on the organization and its people.

When things weren't going right, Level 5 Leaders looked to themselves for the blame; when things were going well, they saw their colleagues and employees as the sources of excellence. At the same time that Al Dunlap was gutting Scott Paper, Darwin Smith was leading its competitor, Kimberly-Clark. Collins has called Smith the very best executive you never heard of. Smith sought no personal attention and pursued a steady strategy to grow his company's business, with Kimberly-Clark eventually coming to own Scott Paper, previously its main competitor, and eventually becoming the number one paper products company in the world. The company today remains first in its industry long after Smith's departure.

Let's leave the business world behind and return to schools. A new principal will be engaged in the process of establishing an ethos from the moment of the very first interview. To whom should our candidate turn for thoughtful advice about the preferred ethos of the principal? It's always a good idea to return to Roland Barth and his basic conception of the principal as a lead learner, which we have seen echoed subsequently by Michael Fullan. The principal who conceives of himself as a continuous learner, rather than an expert, is more likely to inspire his own staff to continuous learning. Barth puts it this way:

> Perhaps the most powerful reason for principals to be learners as well as leaders, to overcome the many impediments to their learning, is the extraordinary influence of modeling behavior. If principals want students and teachers to take learning seriously . . . they must, above all, be head learners. (Barth, 1990, p. 72)

There is no better place for a new principal to start than to remain focused on his own role as a learner and to reflect that back regularly to his staff and community.

UNDERSTANDING YOUR MULTIPLE AUDIENCES

One of the most challenging aspects of being a principal is dealing with so many audiences, each of which has different needs, and each of which usually retains direct access to the principal. The wise principal ought to consider the example of Aristotle, who devoted fully one-third of his *Rhetoric* to discussion and analysis of the audience and its characteristics. On the relationship of the speaker to the audience, Aristotle put it succinctly when he wrote:

> There are three things which inspire confidence in the orator's own character— the three, namely, that induce us to believe a thing apart from any proof of it: good sense, good moral character, and goodwill. (Honeycutt, 2011)

It sounds so simple, doesn't it? Good sense, good moral character, and goodwill combine to form a winning ethos. But just because it's simple doesn't mean it's easy to build an ethos, especially when multiple audiences are involved.

The concept of good sense in a principal might be measured differently by the different audiences to which a principal must respond in any given situation. Suppose, for example, that a high school principal were to lead an initiative that would require students to wear a standard uniform to school each day. In most cases, the principal's internal audience of staff will see the good sense in the proposal, which improves safety and order.

The community's response to school uniforms can run the gamut, and this is where the principal must tread carefully. It costs families less to send their children to school in uniforms than to buy school clothes. School uniforms can also help break down some socioeconomic barriers, and they can help forge a sense of identity in a school. These are all strong arguments, and many families in the community will appreciate them and will see the proposal as a good sense move.

But then there are the students, most of whom will despise a mandatory school uniform. High school is a time for kids to establish their own identity, and what they wear to school is often an important element of that process. Many kids and their families will also see a school uniform proposal as one more example of Big Brother trying to impose crushing conformity. Those kids and those families will see the principal's ethos much differently, and they will attack him.

Let's go back to the entry planning process for a moment. You'll recall that the entry plan involved spending time with people from each of those audiences in order to learn about their hopes and dreams for the school. Doing that entry plan well is how the new principal gets an effective start that prepares him to respond to issues that will emerge over his tenure as the principal. The entry plan helps him to understand his audiences, and it's where he begins to build that ethos he hopes will be characterized by good sense, good moral character, and goodwill.

WHAT YOUR AUDIENCES SEE

The very first impression the principal makes is based on what others actually see. The news media will sometimes refer to this as the "optics" in play, and public relations specialists will work extensively with their clients to make sure that what they look like helps build their ethos. The principal, like the executive, needs to be intentional in his choices if he is to build an ethos that communicates good sense, good moral character, and goodwill. The first thing your audiences see is your clothing, so it makes good sense to be intentional about what you wear. One of the first questions the new principal should address in entry planning is this: Just what is the culture in my new position around what principals wear? School districts develop their own unique cultures around dress, which can vary widely:

- In one district, there is a staff dress code that encourages administrators to wear Hawaiian shirts for about one-third of the year—even at school board meetings.
- In another district, principals may be advised not to dress up for various spirit and costume days. You never know what situation might come in the door at any moment.
- Many districts still want to see principals in highly formal clothing, wearing suits at all times.

Clothing communicates style and status, and it says something about the wearer's formality or informality. Teachers are less burdened by these choices in wardrobe because their primary audience is kids. They wear what makes them and their students feel comfortable. The principal has to figure out how to dress in a way that skirts the lines between what the teachers wear and what the superintendent wears.

For most male principals, that means wearing a nice pair of slacks, a nice dress shirt, and a tie, in school colors if possible. Principals would be wise to spend the vast majority of their clothing budget on shoes because they will walk so much at school. Investing in the most comfortable shoes you can buy is wise; there is nothing worse than a day when your feet are killing you! Female principals should make similar choices—paying particular attention to shoes. Being the principal sometimes begins and ends with the feet. This is no job for wearing the Gucci loafers or the Louboutins. They'll kill your feet, and they'll kill your ethos.

A second element of a principal's optics has to do with his visibility. It is very important to be seen everywhere, even if only for a little while. This is a challenge for the high school principal because there is so much to see, including plays, band reviews, academic competitions, and the beast that is athletics. But that visibility is essential, and the principal simply has to schedule himself so that he does see everything.

The secondary principal needs to make it a point to be everywhere. He should watch after-school practices for all sports, and he should watch every team compete several times each season. He must see every play, every concert, and he must attend every Homecoming dance, every informal dance, and every prom. You would think that all this moving around will wear the principal out, but it doesn't have to. First, the principal quickly learns that he doesn't have to stay for the whole game or the whole dance. At many events, the principal should be the designated greeter for all at the beginning of the event; he then can go home early, leaving the remaining supervision duties to others.

But by far the most important element of a principal's visibility is the amount of time spent in classrooms learning alongside students and staff. It is essential that the principal make it a personal goal to be in every classroom at least once each week, which is challenging as a high school principal, but it is possible. You just have to make it a priority and schedule the time.

Being in classrooms is where the principal both learns and builds an ethos. Here's a simple fact about teachers: they are all, potentially, one step away from being the principal themselves, and they won't trust or respect the principal as a leader if they never see him in their classrooms. There is no substitute for being there alongside the students and staff. The visits can strictly be informal, done without any checklist or mandatory feedback for the teacher. If every visit to a classroom means that each teacher is going to get a note or checklist back from the principal, it will slow down the process of visiting classrooms, and it has the potential to build barriers between the principal and the faculty.

The principal should not be in class each day to evaluate; he should be in class each day to learn alongside his students and staff! A wonderful activity in class is simply to ask students (yes—talk to them!) to tell you what they are working on. Follow-up questions are simple: Is it difficult? What are you learning? Are you getting the help you need? If the class is at a point where the principal could speak to the teacher, he should ask the teacher the same questions. Do this 15 times in a school day, and you build an ethos as a learner and you are completely prepared when a parent contacts you with an instructional issue.

There are other simple rules a principal should adopt regarding visibility that will have an impact on his ethos:

- Don't park your car in a special reserved spot. The principal isn't any more important than anyone else on the staff.
- If your school has carts, don't ride in them. Walk everywhere (it's good exercise) since teachers and kids have to walk everywhere, too.
- During an emergency, don't run. The seconds saved are not worth the potential distress caused in others when they see their principal running.
- Don't walk the campus when school is in session with a cup of coffee in your hand. It sends the wrong message.
- Make it a practice to seldom, if ever, be one of the staff performers in assemblies. Students and teachers are the stars of a school, not the principal.
- The principal doesn't need to use the public address system for announcements. Those can be done by students and staff.

There's another important area where a principal's ethos is tested and developed: responding to a crisis. Every principal will end up responding to crises over the course of his career; they're unavoidable. In a crisis, people want accurate information as quickly as possible, and they want reassurance that they and their students are safe and being cared for. They want to hear that news from the principal. It's important to be present and to be accurate, and it's important that everything be done to ensure that the principal is the single voice, to the extent possible, managing and communicating about the situation.

In the case of an immediate crisis, such as a lockdown, the principal should use the school's public address system to keep students and staff informed. If the principal has adopted the practice of not making announcements over the PA, everyone will know something serious is occurring if the principal's voice comes over the school speakers. Before speaking, jot down the bullet points of what you are going to say on an index card, taking care to keep the content short and direct. Don't speak for more than a minute during those announcements. Also during an immediate crisis, use e-mail to keep staff updated on what is going on. E-mail has the benefit of being somewhat private—as opposed to social media—and it is a good platform to give more detailed information.

Crises are difficult, but they can serve to burnish the principal's reputation as a committed professional who knows what needs to be done. In a crisis, the principal's leadership is essential to the faculty—and especially to the community. Most schools now make use of mass voice mail and e-mail systems that allow the principal to get out a message quickly to all family members. If a message needs to be sent home, it's important that your message get to the home before the students arrive home. Don't wait until dinner to deliver your message; by then there may be all kinds of misinformation floating among students and families. And keep those voice messages short; 45 seconds is a good guideline.

WHAT YOUR AUDIENCES HEAR

If we return to Aristotle's conception of rhetoric for a moment, what he described was that ethos is built by what the audience hears from a speaker. To Aristotle, what the speaker actually says and how he says it matter deeply, a truth that applies to the school principal, which means the principal needs to be thoughtful and intentional about what he says to students, staff, and the community.

When a principal is preparing to speak to the school staff or the larger community, it's important to have a clear message. Write it down! The principal doesn't have to write out every word he intends to say and merely read off a speech, but at a minimum, the principal needs to list the main points he intends to speak about and to then do a simple thing: stick to those points. Wandering off topic confuses audiences. It will also annoy them. Teachers always have something to do, and many would much rather be in their classrooms doing their work than sitting in a staff meeting listening to the principal. Never speak to the staff without an index card in hand outlining your content. That index card will do several things for you:

- It will keep you organized and focused.
- It will keep your content short and to the point.
- It communicates to your audience that you value their time and that your being together matters.
- It signifies your respect.

Another aspect of what your audiences hear has to do with those things the principal says during the day that are not intended for larger audiences. In a word, it is critical that what the principal says in private proves to be a match for what he says in public, both in content and style. The principal who praises his math department in staff meetings and then turns around and trashes them at a district meeting will be found out and will suffer. There is no such thing as a secret in public schools; the principal's hypocrisy will always be found out, if it exists.

WHAT YOUR AUDIENCES READ

Principals write all kinds of things, from website blurbs to employee evaluations, to speeches, to e-mails. They write disciplinary documents, letters of recommendation, and thank-you notes. They send letters to the school and community about wonderful things—and sometimes about tragic things. Those written documents, though, not only communicate information, they also serve to create an ethos, for better or for worse. Some principals write as little as possible; some are not comfortable as writers while others didn't have the time. Some principals fear that their written words in one context could come back to haunt them in another. There are a number of strategies and suggestions the principal can employ in order to be a successful writer:

1. Always visualize your audience before you write. To whom, specifically, are you writing? How do you think your audience is disposed toward your message?

2. Keep the main thing the main thing. Know your main point and get it out there right at the start.
3. Use your own voice. Seriously, failure to write like you speak can make an audience wonder which voice is real or, even worse, who has written the material in the memo.
4. Probably the greatest advice about expository writing ever given comes from Strunk and White's *Elements of Style*, which is "Use less words."
5. Do your best to eliminate (or at least explain) educational jargon. Jargon is epidemic in K–12 education and only seems to get worse. Simplify, simplify.
6. Sarcasm always backfires in writing. Don't use it.
7. The only bigger mistake than sarcasm in writing is profanity. It's indefensible, both in writing and in speech.
8. Always proofread before pressing send. It's easy to get going too fast and to send out something embarrassing.
9. Related to the above rule, ask yourself if you really need to send this memo or e-mail before you do. Sometimes the very best thing to do is to not send that thought in writing, but to instead get up out of your chair and see your potential recipient in person.
10. Don't criticize others in writing. As a principal, you are an encourager. (One exception is disciplinary documents. But just stick to facts in them.)

This is by no means an exhaustive list of strategies the principal should employ as a writer, but it makes a strong start at helping the principal build an ethos of good sense, good moral character, and goodwill. The principals who can build that ethos and live it out in their work each day inevitably end up being successful.

THE FRIDAY LETTER: USING REGULAR WRITING TO BUILD ETHOS AND COMMUNITY

No staff member should ever have to wonder just who the principal is and what he thinks. One way to achieve that goal is simple: write to the staff on a regular basis. For many, writing is the perfect vehicle for communication because many principals actually write better than they speak. Writing also is a great way to attain a new level of understanding about a subject, whether that subject is data analysis or simply a better understanding of your feelings about something.

Forward-thinking school leaders have long advocated for regular writing to staff by the principal. The most famous of these principals was

IN MY EXPERIENCE
10 Years of Friday Letters

In the spring of my seventh year teaching, the principal announced his retirement, and we all began to notice just a little more spring in his step, a little more bounce, and he even took to wearing the occasional polo shirt to work instead of his usually conservative suits and ties. He and I started to speak more, and I came to realize that not knowing him well was a missed opportunity for me to learn. He was smart, clever. He was a man of strong character. He was an excellent principal, and I could have learned so much from him—but I really didn't. Not knowing my principal well had a profound effect on me. I realized that I would have liked him a lot and that I missed valuable learning opportunities. I vowed to myself that if I was ever fortunate to be a school principal, no one would wonder what I thought.

My opportunity to follow through on that vow came in 2006 when I was selected to be the principal of La Sierra High School. Here's the first Friday letter I ever sent to the staff at La Sierra High School:

To: The La Sierra Staff
From: Robert Cunard
Friday, July 28, 2006

THE FRIDAY LETTER

Quote of the Week

"Never doubt that a small group of thoughtful, committed citizens can change the world. Indeed, it is the only thing that ever has."—Margaret Mead

Hello to everyone! I am Robert Cunard, and I have just begun my service as principal here at La Sierra. I have met a few of you in person, but to nearly all of you I am a stranger. We will work on fixing that problem in the days ahead. The purpose of this Friday letter will be to share my thoughts and observations with you every week. I know that many people—especially in a big school like ours—often wonder something like, "Just what does the principal do all day? What does he think? Does he think at all?" My intent will be to answer those questions for you in this weekly note as well as through our work together.

I have always loved the quotation from Margaret Mead which opens this first letter. It's so full of possibility and inspiration. It applies to everyone in our building for a simple reason: we are all here working on changing the world for kids and for our community. Like everyone here, I went into education because I chose to do something meaningful, something that would help others. And like all of you, I quickly learned that by doing something that helped others, my own life took on added meaning and significance. When kids learn, when they grow into the kinds of people we want to be neighbors and friends with, our world is made better. If each of us does what we are called to do here at La Sierra, we really will change the world.

My Bookshelf

I read. From time to time I'll let you know what I'm reading. In preparing myself for this new position, I re-read a book written by Roland Barth called *Improving Schools from Within*. Barth is the founder of the Harvard Principals Center, and some years ago I was fortunate to be in some seminars he presented at UCLA. Barth is a believer that lasting improvement in a school comes from the work of teachers in collaborative groups, and that the mission of the principal is to help a school staff to become a community of learners and leaders. I will be doing my best to uphold Barth's ideals in the months ahead.

The Road Ahead

In this next week, we will complete our hiring process and will focus on opening school in an orderly, effective, efficient manner. As I write this morning, we have one remaining vacancy in science which we should fill next week. The staff have been working hard to get registration materials and processes completed. I have been so impressed with their teamwork and can-do attitude.

I will be completing and sharing an Entry Plan next week. The purpose of the plan is to help me meet people, to hear their suggestions, issues, and perspectives, and to collect some "data" about LSHS. The time-span of that plan will be several months in length because I will have a lot to learn. During this entry phase, I do not intend any substantive changes. We are a strong school, doing very well, and we should continue building on our strengths.

Thanks for welcoming me. Have a great weekend, and enjoy some time with your friends and family.

Robert

As you can see, there was a lot going on in this letter. I was using the letter to introduce myself to a staff that knew nothing of me; most of them hadn't even seen me in person yet. I wrote openly and honestly, in my own voice. In a world where the standard advice to new principals is to attract little attention, I just put it all out there from the start and went to work building relationships with the people in the school and its community.

I'm proud of the body of work in those Friday letters, and I urge every reader of this page to become a writer. You can locate every Friday letter I wrote in those 10 years at http://www.thesuccessfulprincipal.org/friday-letters.html. Feel free to use them for your own inspiration in communicating with your colleagues.

Dennis Littky, who turned around Thayer High School in Winchester, New Hampshire, which ended up being the focus of a successful made-for-TV movie. He went on to create a network of schools known as "The Met," which survive today and are remarkably successful. Littky writes to his staff every Friday. No matter what was going on, he kept in touch every Friday through his Friday letter. Littky's staff never wondered what he thought or who he was; he just put it all out there, every week.

I adopted this practice when I became a principal, and it proved to be a defining feature of my 10 years as a principal.

One of the most important elements of the Friday letter is its regularity, its dependability. Sending a letter every Friday morning is a great way to build an ethos and to consistently communicate a vision. Whether you send the letter on Friday or Monday or any other day, its consistency is powerful. Principals who become weekly writers should also copy district staff as well as fellow principals. You can even send copies to friends and family as a way of keeping in touch.

Here is one cautionary note: once you begin weekly letters, never, ever, miss a Friday. Writing those Friday letters will keep you in constant communication with your staff, your colleagues, and your community. Post them on the school website each week, so the entire universe has access to them. The principal who does this achieves an important goal: no one will ever wonder what he thinks. Over the years, you will encounter staff who don't agree with you, but they will never fail to read the letter, whether they are fans or not. It has impact.

The most important thing weekly writing can do for the principal, though, is that it will help him learn more. That weekly Friday deadline promotes focus and discipline. It will keep the principal reading professional literature as well as other literature. You never knew what revelation might hit each week, but if you aren't actively trying to read something or learn something, the chances of running out of meaningful things to share definitely increase. Some letters will be difficult to write, and a few will be duds. But that's okay; the duds will model the reality of our daily struggle in schools to keep growing ourselves as learners in order to better serve the needs of our students.

CHAPTER 6 KEY POINTS AND STRATEGIES

1. Understand and nurture your ethos. If you don't define it, you can be sure that others will.
2. Everything you say and write, and *how* you say and write it, contributes to your ethos.
3. Always think about your audiences.
4. Strive to be a servant leader and a lead learner.
5. Remember Aristotle: be a principal who projects an ethos of good sense, good moral character, and goodwill.
6. Mind your optics. The principal is always watched.
7. Dress with intention and purpose.
8. Be seen everywhere, but especially in classrooms.

9. Always keep in mind that the students and their teachers are the stars. The principal's job is to support them by being the light that makes others shine brightly.
10. Be calm, clear, and succinct in a crisis.
11. Don't speak off-the-cuff before your faculty or large groups. Write it down.
12. Be a regular writer to your staff and community. People should not wonder what you think.
13. The purpose of regular writing to staff and community is both to communicate and to learn.

Seven

The Empowering Principal

If you want to go fast, go alone. If you want to go far, go together.
—African Proverb

If you want to build a ship, don't drum up people together to collect wood and don't assign them tasks and work, but rather teach them to long for the endless immensity of the sea.—Antoine de Saint-Exupéry

A new position of responsibility will usually show a man to be a far stronger creature than was supposed.—William James

Public school systems are entirely designed to get about 30 children into a well-equipped room with a skilled teacher. Once that's complete, the most important work is done day in and day out by the teachers. And even though the teacher is never really alone, her work can be pretty lonely. She sees very few adults during her work day, has a rushed lunch break of about 20 actual minutes, and struggles to find time even to use the restroom. She does have the benefit of instructional autonomy, great hours, generous benefits, improving pay, and work that is extraordinarily meaningful, but she is usually more alone in her work than her friends who work outside of education. However, the single biggest change in the working life of teachers over the last three decades has been an increase in the number of teachers working in teams to improve student outcomes.

IN MY EXPERIENCE
Teachers Hired 33 Years Apart

I started as an English teacher at George Washington Junior High School in Long Beach, California, back in September 1982, without ever having been interviewed by the school's principal or any sort of committee. I went through a routine screening interview at the central office and received a phone call a few weeks later, 10 days before school was to begin, and was offered my teaching position over the telephone, which I immediately accepted.

I drove to the school, had a brief discussion with the principal, and I was handed a key to my classroom, a copy of the textbooks for seventh-grade and eighth-grade English, and the suggestion that I speak with my department chair if I needed more information. The day before school commenced a department meeting was held where matters pertaining to supplies were discussed, and after less than 30 minutes we broke up and went to get our rooms ready. That was the last department meeting I recall. I was on my own from that point forward. Although I was responsible for teaching English to 180 needy kids, I was most often alone in my work.

Fortunately, things improved over the ensuing decades, and things were much different toward the end of my active career. Contrast my situation with that of a Spanish teacher we hired at Magnolia High School in the summer of 2015. Karen's interview was held at Magnolia High School, and the entire Foreign Language department and I participated in her interview. We selected Karen on the basis of a consensus process.

Once selected, Karen received a raft of materials for the curriculum she was to teach. The department chair and others helped her in getting her room ready. A technology specialist made sure her computer, projector, and other equipment worked. A teacher-leader taught her how to use the Student Information System. She joined a department that met every week during dedicated department time, that wrote common assessments, and that was pretty effective. And I visited her classroom several times a week for the entire year. Karen had a very successful year, in part because she was not isolated.

Even though Karen was doing the same basic work in 2015–2016 as I was doing back in 1982–1983, the conditions under which she was doing it were much different. Although she retained autonomy in terms of instructional methodology and classroom routines, she was very much part of a team, making sure her students learned the same content as all students enrolled in similar Spanish classes and contributing her lesson ideas to her department during its meetings and in dozens of private discussions with colleagues. Not only did Karen's students do very well, her contributions ended up impacting the work of her colleagues for the better.

WHY TEAMS?

American public schools were long organized under a factory model, and they came to be remarkably similar across our vast country. Ted Sizer put it well when he described our high schools back in 1984:

> Over the years a set of conventions about how to "keep high school" has emerged and is now so familiar that it is rarely questioned. . . . The curriculum is the long shadow of departments classified as English, mathematics, science, social studies, physical education, and so forth. The coinage in school is valued by time spent—the 53-minute period, the year ("four years of English"), and "units" completed. (Sizer, 1984, p. 34)

We kept up this factory metaphor by which we organized schools in the last century because it made sense. Factories were the engine of American prosperity and many Americans worked in them and admired them, so it made sense that we replicated factories in our schooling systems. Leslie Hart summed up factory model schools, their history and design, and their limitations when he wrote:

> Almost a century and a half ago, Horace Mann began popularizing a much-modified version of a system of schooling he had briefly observed in Prussia. Factories were then widely admired, and Mann offered what was plainly a batch-processing, avowedly factory school, built on the class and grade principle. From the outset it worked poorly to produce learning, as the literature shows. Young humans just do not process well as raw material for a factory. Perversely, they have refused to learn in the same way, on the same schedule, and to the same depth. (Hart, 1989, p. 239)

For decades, schools operated intentionally as cultural institutions that sorted and selected students. How well one did in school determined if one might go to college (winner) or directly into the workforce (loser), most likely consigned to physically rigorous or menial work. Since our economy demanded large numbers of unskilled and semi-skilled workers, this sorting and selecting actually advanced societal needs. It wasn't a bad thing that about one-third of students dropped out, about one-third graduated with some skills, and one-third graduated ready to go to college. The schools we had fit the needs of the times in which we lived.

But starting in the 1980s, the needs of our society changed. Factory employment shrank as automation took over human jobs. Foreign competition led to increased productivity demands on American industry. Our country transformed in a short period of time from an industrial economy to an information-based economy, and this created a need for a different kind of workforce; a more educated, literate, and technologically sophisticated workforce became an essential element of the economy. A community that can't produce that kind of workforce is going to suffer, which is precisely what happened in the middle-American rust belt.

At the same time our educational needs were changing, our investment in schools stagnated, or even declined in real terms, as was the case in California and many other portions of our country. It became the challenge of schools to somehow achieve better learning results for all students while spending less money than before. Today our challenge is to ensure that every student not only graduates from high school, but that they all graduate college and be career ready. This is a goal never before achieved on earth, and yet every school across America is now doggedly pursuing it.

How are schools supposed to do more than they ever had done while using less resources than they've ever had? The answer is that we were forced to innovate, to unleash our creativity and to get more productivity out of each person in the building. That's what business has done and, after some time lag, that is the strategy schools eventually adopted. Teamwork is cheap, and it turns out to be effective. And best of all, teamwork best serves our students and has the enviable benefit of improving the satisfaction of team members. Michael Fullan puts it this way:

> Humans are fundamentally motivated by two factors: doing things that are intrinsically meaningful to themselves, and working with others—peers, for example—in accomplishing goals never before reached. (Fullan, 2014, p. 7)

That's why we are working so hard in schools to put teachers into high-functioning teams: we are trying to accomplish goals never before reached. And of course, now that student learning results in schools are public, we are trying to achieve these difficult goals under a great deal of scrutiny and stress. We'll never get all students college and career ready if we return to the era of teacher autonomy and indifference that characterized the 1980s. We don't run schools that way now because it simply won't meet our economy's needs and would ill serve our communities. Schools face demands for continuous improvement, just like businesses. The principal's best hope for continuous improvement in her school is through putting teams in place that become self-managing engines of improvement.

TEAM BUILDING 101: COACH YOUR TEAMS

No matter what the team, a sense of basic order and purpose are essential to its effectiveness. One of the principal's key roles in school leadership is to serve as the head coach for each team. In this instance, school athletics is an excellent metaphor for the relationship between a principal and one of her teams. In athletics, the coach never takes the field. Instead, she provides her team with the time and support they require in order to perform their best. The coach is acutely aware that there are limits to what she can do as the coach. She provides the team with resources, creates time and space for their work (practice), provides feedback when appropriate, and ultimately sits on the sideline when they play their games, providing occasional tactical advice.

The coach can only intrude so much during games, because the team needs time and space to play, to figure things out. A great coach knows that her players will grow as they figure things out for themselves through their shared work together. Just like athletic teams, the teams our principal establishes in her school need specific forms of support and guidance if they are to become high functioning:

Mission

A team without a clear sense of its mission isn't really a team. It's a collection of friends or colleagues, but it's not a team. Rick DuFour (2006) may have put it best in his definition of a Professional Learning Community (PLC)—just another form of a team—which he called a group of people working interdependently to achieve a common goal for which they are mutually accountable. Teams exist to do work that makes a difference—work that improves student achievement and the lives of its members. As the principal puts together the teams in her school, it's critical to clarify the purpose of each team and for that purpose to remain at the front and center of each team's work. If the purpose is ultimately fulfilled or becomes irrelevant to improving student achievement or the orderly operation of the school, then the team should disband. After all, teachers are all busy; they hate nothing more than having their time wasted in a meeting without purpose.

A Designated Leader

Somebody has to conduct the orchestra. Every team needs some sort of designated leader or chair. Someone has to make sure the agenda is done, that snacks are taken care of, that there's a place to meet. Most important, our principal needs to be able to identify and work with the leaders of teams to monitor their work. It's not so much an issue of accountability as it is an issue of efficiency. Depending on the team, it may be that formal leaders are already in place (e.g., department chairs, grade level leaders, head counselors) or that the group will first need to select a chair. Either way, it must be clear by the close of a team's first meeting who will be serving as its leader. If this isn't done, the team will collapse. In the case where a principal is creating a new team to address a challenge, it may be wise to have a co-administrator serve as chair, at least at the start.

Time

Time is the coin of the realm in schools. Finding time within the contracted day for a team to meet is essential if the team is to stick to its mission and work throughout a school year. Thankfully, many schools have developed innovative scheduling systems that now provide regular meeting time within the school day. One of the things that will challenge the principal is just how to divvy up those meeting opportunities so that there is equity and the school's teamwork does not intrude too much on the core mission of teaching.

It is important to avoid holding meetings after school. First, everyone's tired after school, and even occasionally snappy. After school everyone has something else to do or something else on their mind. Here's a challenge: the next time you find yourself in an after-school meeting, look around at all the teachers who are parents of younger children. They are already twice as tired as everyone else, and now they have the added stress of trying to manage picking up their children, preparing dinner late, or any of a thousand other things that disrupt the routines of their family life. Even if you have the right to call after school meetings, you should find better times to meet.

Lunchtime meetings are also extremely difficult and should be avoided. First, lunch is pretty short. In California, a teacher's lunch from exit bell to teaching her next class is 35 minutes in most secondary schools. By the time your teachers get food, make it to the meeting site, and get settled, you're lucky if you have 15 good minutes. However, some lunch meetings may prove successful. If the principal needs to meet with a group at lunch, she must first be sure they are all willing to do so and that a lunch meeting is what they prefer.

Second, to maximize meeting time and to make it a nice environment, provide lunch for the team meeting. Yes, out of your personal funds. Prior to a lunch meeting, pick up whatever you have ordered from a local restaurant and set up a buffet in a conference room or empty classroom. Team members should know that your lunch meetings feature food (and what food is coming) so they don't have to pack their own lunch. They will arrive quickly, happy to be eating something nicer than a typical teacher's lunch. The other useful facet of a lunch meeting is its short time frame. You still have, at best, 20 minutes of time, so the agenda has to be efficient and limited. The principal must not forget that the faculty, like Napoleon's army, marches on its stomachs.

Another meeting choice available is a full paid day, either during the summer or while released from teaching, with classes covered by substitutes. This is a good option for team meetings on occasion if a team has a long task to complete. But be forewarned: releasing teachers from their instructional day has hidden costs because it means their students are taught by less qualified teachers! In a high school setting, especially, substitutes mostly assign work and monitor students; they often are incapable of providing any instruction in the subject they may be assigned to cover on a given day. That hurts students, and our purpose in school is to help students!

If possible, the principal should arrange for the use of paid work days over the summer break as a way of providing teams time to complete big projects. Those days are more expensive since paying a teacher for even four hours a day at her hourly rate exceeds the cost to a school of her substitute. Regardless of which time works best for specific teams, the principal must be thoughtful and strategic about providing her teams with the right time to do their work. It's an important decision.

Norms

Once a team is established, the very first thing it needs to do is to establish its norms. The wise principal should insist that every team creates norms, writes them down, reviews them periodically, and then abides by

---

IN MY EXPERIENCE
The Value of Norms

When we began to establish the Professional Learning Community model at La Sierra High School, our experts from the County Office insisted that every team write norms and bring them back to the Leadership Team for discussion. The Leadership Team also wrote norms. Somewhere in my head, I thought this was kind of artificial, perhaps even slowing down the work on which we needed to focus. But I came to see things differently after just a few weeks when I visited the PLC meeting of the Visual and Performing Arts (VAPA) Department. No department was more challenged by the PLC system than VAPA. Its teachers were brilliant artists, musicians, and directors. They were also iconoclasts and mostly did not like one another.

Sara, their department chair, was genuinely worried that her meetings would dissolve into out-and-out conflict. But Sara was tough, and she cared about the school and improving it. At the team's first meeting, all they did was work on norms. At the second meeting, one of the artists brought in a nice, laminated table tent, which listed the agreed-upon norms. It was placed in the center of the table around which they sat, and it was agreed that if a norm was being violated the only action anyone would take would be to simply point at the table tent. And this simple system worked. These iconoclasts managed to hold successful meetings for two years. They didn't all become better friends, but they did become a better department. I don't think it would have happened without norms.

them. You would think that a group of educated professionals could skip this step and get right to work, but experience suggests otherwise. Norms create boundaries, expectations, and safety; they are comforting.

Communication and Record Keeping

Once you unleash your teams and they get to work fulfilling their mission, you have to have a system in place to keep records. The principal must expect every team to publish an agenda in advance of its meeting, to write down the proceedings and decisions arrived at during the meeting, and to share those things with the school leadership. In Leadership Team meetings, the principal will be able to devote more and more time to allow PLCs and other teams to update everyone on their work. Those discussions with the Leadership Team are essential to keep the school on a unified mission, rather than behaving as a collection of departments pursuing a series of separate agendas. The principal needs to specify in advance just how much record keeping is necessary and then work with team leaders to ensure that it gets done and that it is adequately communicated across the campus.

Autonomy

If you want to unleash the power and creativity of your teams, you have to provide them with enough autonomy. Teachers are incredibly creative, as a group. Sadly, much of that creativity was stifled during the No Child Left Behind (NCLB) era from which we are still emerging. Your teams need to know that while their "what" (achieving their mission) may be fixed, their "how" should not be limited. So when the leader of a team comes to you with a new idea for the "how" of improving student achievement, your job isn't to poke holes in it. Rather, your job is to help the team enact its vision by doing whatever you can to make it easier.

The principal's challenge is that granting sufficient autonomy to teams means that she will occasionally end up having to justify practices that are big departures from previous systems and norms. But she has to do it if she wants to achieve great results. If we are called to make all students college and career ready—and we are—then we are going to have to use different strategies than what we have used previously. Those new strategies are more likely to emerge from teams that are granted autonomy over the "how."

THE ADMINISTRATIVE TEAM—HEART OF YOUR SYSTEMS

No team will prove more important to the principal's sanity and the day-to-day operation of her school than the administrative team. The administrative team is the one that meets most often, weekly in many settings, and it is the team that manages the routines and procedures of keeping school. This team is small, includes all site administrators, and will also include key program leaders. The administrative team should meet every Monday morning right before school. In a high school setting, it should be composed of the following:

- Principal
- All assistant principals
- Head counselor
- Intervention coordinator
- Athletic director
- Activities director

This meeting should be purposeful, but short, seldom running for more than 40 minutes. There must always be a written agenda. This is an operations meeting where you will do everything from planning out weekly supervision, to preparing for assemblies, to managing the school's scheduling and testing processes. All these employees are extraordinarily busy people, but this meeting is essential. The administrative team meeting is where you formally make sure each week that you are ready for whatever is coming up next.

At first glance, the principal might be tempted to not have this meeting, reasoning that the operations work of the school can be accomplished without sitting down together about 35 times in a school year. However, absent that regular meeting, the principal will end up holding a lot of individual discussions with those same individuals who would otherwise sit with her every Monday during the team meeting. Those individual discussions will take more time than the Monday meeting, and may occur during times the principal prefers to be in classrooms. Co-administrators who work in schools without those weekly meetings can come to feel just a little in the dark about certain things. Another benefit of this weekly team meeting is that it gives the principal an opportunity to benefit from the synergy of this group while planning out the routines of school.

THE MANAGEMENT TEAM—YOU AND YOUR ADMINISTRATORS

The management team in a school is the label for a very small group: the principal and her assistant principals. The way the management team functions and relates to one another is essential to the principal's daily sense of well-being and, ultimately, to the operation of the school. In a secondary school setting, there are many jobs to do, and the way to ensure that they get done efficiently is to create a chart that clearly delineates just who is responsible for what things.

The principal should revise the chart every summer, depending on the school's needs and the growth needs of her co-administrators. She should structure the annual evaluation of her co-administrators around their attainment of goals they write in relation to their duties. That duty list should also be published to all school staff so that they know who to contact if they have an issue that requires attention.

The real purpose of the list is to empower co-administrators to own their areas of responsibility. A secondary purpose of the list is to ensure that the school will continue to run smoothly if the principal has to be away. The reality of the contemporary school principal, sadly, is that she can expect to be away from her campus up to 20 percent of the time school is actually in session; in some districts, the figure is even higher.

Even though the management team may never have a formal meeting, they should be a team that meets more than any team in school by doing one incredibly simple thing: eating a private lunch together every day. The principal and her co-administrators simply must stop what they're doing every day, sit down together, and just eat lunch. In the schools where this is a regular practice, the management team will be tight and together; in those where this is less common, the management team members may pursue their own ends.

The real purpose of lunch together is simply to become better friends. After all, the administrators are the only employees in the building who can be transferred or dismissed at will on any given day. They are the only employees with no stated hours, and their position description always concludes with the phrase, "Other duties as assigned." They are ultimately responsible for everything in the school, and yet they possess the lowest levels of safety and security in their positions. They need each other, and they are terribly busy all day at school; those 20 minutes at lunch are essential.

THE LEADERSHIP TEAM—WHERE BIG ISSUES GET DISCUSSED

The Leadership Team is a big group. It should include everyone from the Administrative Team and all academic department chairs. It should also include the school psychologist and any teachers on special assignments. Leadership Team meetings may have as many as 25 participants. This meeting is where you discuss bigger issues. This is the group that will take on everything from professional development planning to testing procedures to the structure of the school's master schedule.

The challenge in running a Leadership Team meeting with this many participants is to keep the agenda short, participation meaningful, and communication wide open. The Leadership Team should meet once a month. The principal should develop the agenda in advance for each meeting, and it should circulate prior to the meeting. Keep things short, with the meeting length running less than an hour. That means that the agenda really can't have more than four items on it if you are to give each item due attention. Minutes must be taken at each meeting, and they should be e-mailed to the entire staff as soon as possible, usually the next day.

The Leadership Team is a working group, a thinking group. When the Leadership Team approaches a problem, discusses it, and is able to reach consensus about the best course of action after thoroughly exploring a variety of alternatives, it will improve the school. Using the Leadership Team this way means that big decisions don't have to rest entirely on the principal's shoulders. It also means that there is a way for all voices to be heard when you are working on something of school-wide importance.

The final essential element of the Leadership Team is to never have votes. All decisions must be made on the basis of consensus, which is best defined as existing when all voices have been heard and the will of the group is apparent. Consensus building can take time, which means that it may take several meetings to get something off the agenda and put into action, but it is worthwhile. A benefit to consensus building, as opposed to simply voting, is that there are no losers when a group reaches consensus. Since everyone has participated, all voices have been heard, and the will of the group is clearly evident, you should never get stuck in a situation where an action taken as a result of a Leadership Team decision gets sandbagged by others.

THE PROFESSIONAL DEVELOPMENT TEAM

An effective, improving school must have a team devoted to the ongoing professional development of the faculty. Sometimes the Leadership Team becomes the group that attends to professional development if the school is organized into PLCs. Leadership Team meetings in schools that have a strong PLC system in place often become the venue where each PLC team leader shares her team's SMART (Strategic, Measurable, Attainable, Results-oriented, Time-bound) goals and progress. If a PLC needs professional development beyond the PLC process, the Leadership Team can become the place for that to be discussed and dealt with.

Another way to attend to professional development is to form a teacher-led Professional Development Committee. This group can be chaired by an instructional coach or a teacher on special assignment. Each academic department or grade level should provide one teacher who will participate in the Professional Development Committee. This committee can become one of the school's primary engines of academic improvement if they were given autonomy and control of something very important: dedicated staff meeting time.

The Professional Development Committee can be tasked with planning out a year-long arc of professional learning for the entire faculty, making use of those regular meetings. They also may be empowered (and funded) to release teachers for a day to do Learning Walks across the campus, observing their colleagues and learning more about what strong instructional practices on the campus in other departments look like.

Teachers on a high-functioning Professional Development Committee will prove to be a powerful group. They are often inspired learners themselves. This committee can become a collection of stars, and the principal's best move may be to attend the meetings when possible, support their initiatives, and model professional learning herself. If a principal's job is to do whatever she can to help her faculty grow, then empowering this committee may well turn out to be one of the very best strategies she can enact.

DEPARTMENTAL OR GRADE-LEVEL TEAMS: THE NITTY-GRITTY OF PLCs

The teams in school that do the most work directly affecting instruction are departmental, course-alike, or grade-level PLC teams. Entire books have been written about the PLC process and unleashing its power to improve student achievement. The very best guide for supporting the work of those PLCs is *Learning by Doing: A Handbook for Professional Learning Communities at Work*, written by Richard DuFour, Rebecca DuFour, Robert Eaker, and Thomas Many (2006). This volume includes all the support any PLC will ever need, from defining its purpose to learning to collaborate to growing the PLC process beyond the small group. The volume is meant to be used as both a reference and a workbook. The principal leading a school committed to PLC groups would be wise to buy copies for all Leadership Team members and to work through its various phases together.

The principal's real challenge in dealing with PLCs across her campus is this: she needs to ensure that each PLC is pursuing a goal that is strategic and specific, measurable, attainable, oriented toward an academic result for students, and specifically time bound. In a high school with perhaps a dozen different PLCs or more, this monitoring can be a challenge, which is why she must assign supervision and support of academic departments to assistant principals as well as herself. Each administrator should look after two or three departments, sit in on their PLC meetings periodically, and support the team leaders as necessary in the PLC process. Once the process is up and running, the school's administration should have a very light hand on the tiller, and perhaps not be steering things at all if the teams are truly high functioning.

TASK FORCES—WHEN YOU'VE GOT A JOB TO DO

Sometimes short-term needs emerge in a school that requires the formation of a team to do some investigating or to make recommendations. Calling these short-term groups task forces emphasizes that their work is important but limited in scope. A task force does work designed to inform the rest of the staff. It's wise for the principal to employ a task force for the purpose of evaluating something controversial. When the grumbling about a program, procedure, or routine grows loud enough so that it must be addressed, the formation of a task force to start the work is an ideal method.

A task force should be led by an assistant principal, and it should be charged with reviewing the efficacy of the program at issue, reviewing the literature around the program, and visiting other schools implementing the program or who have developed a different method to address the problem at hand. A task force must be given several specific things to do and a deadline to present its findings to the faculty. Ideally, a task force must include people on both sides of the issue, so that its findings aren't open to charges of bias. The task force should present its findings to the faculty in a written report and through a presentation at a staff meeting.

Once the task force completes its work, it becomes time for the Leadership Team to wrestle with its findings and to ultimately take action. Again, the best way to arrive at a decision is through consensus. Using the task force in this manner can be a very successful choice for the principal. Its work is controlled by its members, is usually quite thorough, and removes any possible thought that the principal somehow dictates its results.

CONFLICT AND OUTLIERS

Once you put teachers into teams and ask them to work together to achieve a common goal, some conflict will be bound to emerge. Even high-functioning teams will occasionally be challenged by low-level conflict.

The nature of the teacher's employment security makes it easier for some to engage in conflict. Most teachers in a public school building have lifetime job security, and that very security can make it easier for some to follow their baser instincts. You'll always find a few teachers on any given campus who are simply lazy and resist doing "extra" work, and you may find more than a few who are just vain. When these individuals end up in PLC teams, there is a tendency to let them miss the meetings or to attend without actively participating.

It's easy to believe that PLC meetings will go so much better if only that one teacher—call him Fred—were excused from the meetings. Fred might arrive late, bring a negative vibe, or even demonstrate complete inattention. In the private sector, Fred might soon be out of a job, but in most schools, Fred has a lifetime appointment. How should our principal handle these situations?

Conflict and outliers really test the principal's leadership. While the principal does have the power to direct Fred to attend the meeting and to participate as a professional team member and to issue disciplinary documents if he does not do so, this command and control kind of management is not as effective as a different strategy: building a relationship with Fred and finding out what makes him tick.

There are Freds in every school, and the principal simply must refuse to let them skip out on PLC work for one simple reason: it is in the best interest of the entire school that every teacher be an active PLC participant. Some Freds will undoubtedly tell the principal that they dislike the meetings because they aren't learning anything and they already have the best strategies, the best results, or a special system that works for them. If that were true, then Fred needs to be sharing that with his colleagues during the meetings so that they and their students will benefit.

More often, though, Fred just doesn't want to work differently than he did the day, week, or years before. He knows it, and the principal knows it, and he knows the principal knows it. In order to get Fred to be present and involved, the principal needs to be a regular presence in his classroom, and he and the principal need to be talking with each other about how his students are doing. Everything comes back to that one simple fact: How are your students doing? When you frame things in that manner repeatedly, Fred is going to attend the meeting, perhaps begrudgingly, but he'll be there. Once there, a team with norms, a clear purpose, and a goal specifically related to student achievement is going to slowly win Fred over. It happens more often than you think.

CHAPTER 7 KEY POINTS AND STRATEGIES

1. The old model of school as a factory where some swim and others sink is finished. In order to get all students proficient, we must unleash our creativity and power through teamwork.
2. The most powerful work in schools is being led by teacher-leaders.
3. As principal, your most important job is to coach your team leaders.

4. Teams all need:
   - a clear mission
   - a designated leader
   - protected time to meet and work
   - clear, written norms
   - communication and record-keeping systems
   - autonomy
5. The Administrative Team and its weekly meeting are essential for the orderly operation of the school.
6. The Management Team must be tight and ought to be friends. Eat lunch together every time you can.
7. The Leadership Team should only take on a few issues during its monthly meetings and should be a consensus-building body.
8. The Professional Development team can be a powerful engine to improve student achievement.
9. PLC teams should operate under the processes outlined in *Learning by Doing* (DuFour et al., 2006).
10. A task force can be a valuable tool for taking on a challenging issue.
11. Expect conflict and outliers when teachers work in teams.
12. It is better to persuade outliers than to command them.

Eight

The Motivating Principal

Work isn't to make money; you work to justify life.—Marc Chagall

The one thing that matters is the effort. It continues, whereas the end to be attained is but an illusion of the climber, as he fares on and on from crest to crest; and once the goal is reached it has no meaning.—Antoine de Saint-Exupéry

If your actions inspire others to dream more, learn more, do more and become more, you are a leader.—John Quincy Adams

The school principal's success and that of his students is directly related to the degree of motivation unleashed in the staff at his school. A motivated, engaged staff will work harder, call in sick less often, collaborate more effectively, and be more likely to change the lives of students for the better. The question of what motivates people to effort is a critical one, though, and it is useful to understand motivation from a bigger perspective than one that simply describes tips and tricks to inspire people to work harder and happier.

Before our society organized into urban and suburban cores dominated by commerce, motivation to work was a simple thing: one worked in order to have food, shelter, and safety. In an agrarian society, people worked to fulfill their most basic biological needs. Commerce and currency were merely more efficient means to ends that supported the agrarian enterprise. Some things were just too hard to create at home, and it made more sense to buy them from tradesmen. Preindustrial America was defined by our Protestant work ethic because our forefathers simply *had* to work all the time in order to grow food, harvest it, and meet those most basic needs. The American character was shaped by the challenges of our new country and just how difficult it was to make a life across so much of it.

As we industrialized and grew our urban and suburban areas, we created a new kind of worker who toiled in factories, mines, and businesses. Because their work was no longer so intimately connected to providing their own food, these industrial age employees lacked the same basic motivation to work as did their agrarian forbears. Doing one's work in a factory, mine, or shop with limited motivation didn't necessarily mean that the employee ultimately was less well fed, clothed, or sheltered.

With basic biological motivation less in play in these new workplaces, business owners needed new ways to motivate employees, and they eventually settled on a very simple formula: the application of extrinsic (outside of the person) rewards and punishments. Frederick Taylor, the founder of the scientific management movement, studied workers and their productivity in the workplace, starting with time and motion studies and moving on to systems for rewarding improved productivity, and thereby punishing less productive workers.

The work of Taylor and others in the early 20th century was built on the principle that people were economic animals and would do what they could to maximize earnings. This led to things like piecework and production targets and, ultimately, a Darwinian system where the strongest, most reliable, most productive workers thrived. Work was still very routine for many, requiring little creativity in most settings, so the basic carrots (rewards) and sticks (punishments) system prevailed as the motivational method for generations of industrial workers.

Carrots and sticks worked well enough in an age where many were employed in routine work in shops and on factory floors. So did Horace Mann's industrial age schools. Those schools produced people who could read and perform rudimentary mathematics, and those skills were sufficient enough with which to build a life for most of the last century. But the world has truly changed, and the use of carrots and sticks does not apply well today in a workplace where jobs are not routine, and what we ask our staff to do in schools today is far from routine.

The work of a teacher is complex and constantly challenging. The best teachers experience continuous growth over the arc of a career. No amount of carrots or sticks is needed to motivate them to continue their quests for improved performance; they'll do it themselves. We are blessed with teachers everywhere who work like crazy for relatively modest pay, foregoing the luxuries their fellow college graduates often enjoy. Somehow, those finest teachers develop an intrinsic (inside themselves) motivation that animates their work for a lifetime. That's what our principal should be trying to tap into in his school. To understand what ignites these star performers, we're going to take an extended look at two of the great writers on motivation: Viktor Frankl and Daniel Pink.

MOTIVATION—EVEN INSIDE A CONCENTRATION CAMP

Viktor Frankl's *Man's Search for Meaning: An Introduction to Logotherapy* (1984) can be a challenging book to study for school administrators.

It can be difficult for them to see how a man's tale of survival in Nazi concentration camps, which occupies two-thirds of the volume, would in any way help them become better school administrators. But this little volume spells out some key ideas about the human condition, and its message is powerful and incisive.

Prior to his imprisonment, Viktor Frankl was a physician in Vienna. He developed a deep interest in mental health and became a psychiatrist, working in Vienna at the same time Freud was doing his work. Where Freud saw neurosis as emanating from struggles to reconcile elements of one's past, Frankl took a much different view, believing instead that neurosis and most mental illness resulted from a person's failure to find and make meaning in his life. He began a practice he called logotherapy, as opposed to Freud's psychotherapy.

One of the most striking things about Frankl's concentration camp narrative is that he discovered something remarkable during his imprisonment: even in the harshest, most abysmal circumstances possible, certain prisoners managed to keep up their motivation. In the face of constant suffering, deprivation, and degradation, these people survived. Somehow, they found meaning and purpose, even in suffering. The stresses placed on these people did not break them; rather, they were strengthened. Frankl likened this to a phenomenon in engineering:

> If architects want to strengthen a decrepit arch, they increase the load which is laid upon it, for thereby the parts are joined more firmly together. (Frankl, 1984, p. 110)

Following his imprisonment, Frankl further developed and described the basic principles of logotherapy, which takes the view that every person is engaged in a search for meaning in his life through the pursuit of three avenues to meaning:

1. Creating a work, or doing deeds (work);
2. Experiencing something or encountering someone (love);
3. In the face of a fate one cannot change, rising above oneself, or changing oneself (enduring).

Once that sense of meaning emerges in his life, a person can be healthy. In contrast to the popular notion from psychotherapy that people are in search of an equilibrium and a stressless situation, Frankl developed a therapeutic model built around helping people seek purpose. That effort to seek purpose and to live with it in mind will create some tension, but that is just what man needs:

> What man needs is not a tensionless state, but rather the striving and struggling for a worthwhile goal. (1984, p. 110)

In Frankl's view, the school principal is confronted with a staff that includes some people who are struggling because they have lost that sense of the meaning of their work, even perhaps their life. The loss of this sense of purpose has serious effects in schools and society. In schools, we used to call this sense of ennui teacher burnout. More properly, Frankl urges us to view this through a different lens, reminding us that many who suffer do so because of an underlying existential vacuum. Frankl's vision of man should have a profound impact on a school principal. Over the course of a career, the principal will see three kinds of people on every faculty:

1. More than a few teachers face existential crises that affect their performance and motivation. These burned-out teachers coast along, doing enough to get their jobs done, but showing little passion or initiative in their work.
2. Most teachers have found their sense of purpose in their work. They show up every day, and they work pretty hard.
3. A few teachers in every school will be transcendent in their work ethic, their motivation, and their love of their work and the students.

The principal who has a down day himself needs to get out of his office and go watch those star teachers as a way of recovering his own sense of meaning and purpose. The stars bring no existential crises to work; their purpose is clear and their classrooms transformative places. The kids all know who those teachers are, and they gravitate toward them, whether it is to work in their classrooms at lunch or after school, to join the club they sponsor, or to play on the teams they coach. Just like Frankl said, stressing the systems of these stars only makes them shine brighter.

FROM CARROTS AND STICKS TO DRIVE

In 2009, writer Daniel Pink published *Drive: The Surprising Truth about What Motivates Us*, which became a runaway best seller. Pink kept finding models and systems that defied industrial age notions about extrinsic motivation. The 21st century revealed people everywhere who were supremely motivated and doing big things absent any extrinsic motivators, often for free. For instance, Wikipedia, the crowd-sourced online encyclopedia edited entirely by volunteers, dethroned Microsoft's Encarta. Unpaid programmers all over the world created the free, open-sourced Linux operating system, which now runs computers worldwide. How could this possibly happen in a rational economic system? Why would people do so much work for free?

Pink began looking for answers as he studied a variety of businesses that seemed to have tapped into successful motivational strategies other than carrots and sticks. He discovered that social science research had developed a clear literature, which noted that extrinsic rewards were often counterproductive, actually reducing worker productivity and contributing to unhealthy anxiety.

On the other hand, there were places where employees were achieving great productivity through *intrinsic* motivation and experiencing great satisfaction at work. Places like 3M and the Best Buy corporate offices devised practices that freed their workers from their routines, from time clocks, even from the offices themselves. Pink saw a revolution in the making, as progressive companies tapped into new kinds of managerial strategies. The absence of extrinsic goals in these settings did not mean that employees worked without direction; rather, they began to have more opportunity to set and own their direction, which proved to be a highly effective management strategy.

Pink learned that the emerging field of positive psychology had developed a clear understanding of the three factors that motivate human beings:

1. sufficient *autonomy* to act with choice;
2. striving for *mastery*; and
3. a clear sense of *purpose*.

Pink found companies, such as Atlassian, that let employees spend 20 percent of their work hours on projects of their own devising. At the Best Buy corporate offices, he found a Results-Only Work Environment, which unchained employees from their offices and traditional working hours. Given this autonomy and trust, employees in these companies thrived, and businesses caught on, as Pink notes:

> [T]he shrewdest enterprises afford employees the freedom to sculpt their jobs in ways that bring a little bit more flow to otherwise mundane activities. (Pink, 2009, p. 119)

The idea of experiencing the state of flow at work gets to the notion of mastery, the second of the three big motivators. Pink teaches us that mastery has three embedded elements:

1. Mastery is a mind-set.
2. Mastery is a pain, not easily achieved.
3. Mastery is an asymptote, never exactly reached, but closely approached.

Everyone has those moments where great effort and experience suddenly coincide and productivity, happiness, and satisfaction soar. The psychologist Mihaly Csikszentmihalyi (1990) studied the psychological concept he ultimately labeled as flow, performing the fundamental research behind it. What he discovered is that flow doesn't just have to occur at rare moments, it is something that is more likely to occur under the right conditions. An enterprise, be it a business, a classroom, or any kind of organization that brings people together for a shared purpose, can be tuned to help its members more easily and frequently achieve flow states.

The final key element to motivation is purpose, which sounds a whole lot like Frankl's search for meaning, doesn't it? It turns out that some purposes prove more motivating than others. Pink reports on the findings of a long-term study of graduates from the University of Rochester. The researchers interviewed students as they were preparing to graduate from college and asked them about their levels of happiness and their goals for the future.

Years later, they tracked those graduates down and reinterviewed them to see how they had fared. The researchers found that people who were moving toward a long-term goal and were on track were happier than they'd been as college students. In contrast, the researchers found that people who were in pursuit of *financial* goals, even if they were achieving them, were less happy than they had been as college students. Their identified purpose wasn't big enough or meaningful enough to lead to happiness.

Fortunately, the principal's target audiences in school (himself, the staff, and the students) are in school each day with the opportunity to fulfill extraordinarily meaningful purposes. And though we may not be able to allow our students and our staff as much freedom from their classrooms as was given to those employees at Best Buy, there are things we can do in school that will tap into the lessons uncovered by Frankl and Pink, and it is to that which we now turn.

MOTIVATING ONESELF

Let's return to the place called school and examine what the principal can do within his sphere in order to impact motivation. A principal has the necessary power and influence to impact the motivation of three key constituents in his school: himself, the staff, and the student body. We begin here with an important constituent: the principal himself. As we've already seen, school principals often receive little to no direct personal support from their supervising district-level administrators. Let's explore how the principal can impact his own motivation through the lenses of purpose, autonomy, and mastery.

Ordinarily it's assumed that everyone who leads and teaches in schools has a clear sense of purpose, but that's not always true. Some teachers and administrators end up fulfilling a purpose as limited as just getting to Friday. Seriously. Some administrators view the purpose of their work as merely being about advancement to the next rung in the hierarchy. Those aren't compelling reasons to get up in the morning and go to school with energy and your best effort; they're a recipe for cruising at work, drinking coffee in your office. That's why it's important that the principal take some time to clearly identify his purpose in his work, to write it down, and to periodically check in on his progress toward achieving that stated purpose.

One possible statement of purpose for a school principal is to lead his school in such a way that student achievement steadily improves and that the work lives of the staff become happier, more interesting, and more fulfilling. You'll notice that this purpose is not easily measurable, which is fine. Not everything that matters can be reduced to a metric. The principal will end up with plenty of concrete goals supplied for the school in the School Plan, so it's all right to be broad and non-metric in identifying purpose. It's critical that the principal know at his core what purpose he's trying to fulfill and that he check in on that purpose regularly.

We've seen that the principal has less autonomy than outsiders think, but that doesn't mean he can't exert some of it in order to meet his own needs for growth. The principal can address his autonomy needs through investment in his own personal and professional development. He can volunteer to serve on school accreditation teams, which will take him off-site several days each school year.

The choice to write Friday letters every week of the school year also helps him with autonomy since it requires him to process the work of the school and to constantly refine his own voice to the staff and community about what the school is doing and how well. Sure, it is "extra" work, but each week when he sits down to that blank document, he begins anew to put in writing his own interpretation of how the school is doing. It is a lot of work, but it keeps the work interesting, and doing it will keep him a bit more autonomous than many fellow principals. They get stuck with just data; weekly writing enables a principal to look at many other things and gives him a chance to revisit his purpose.

Even though mastery is an asymptote, never really attainable, it is crucial for the principal to step back and measure things and to report on progress every so often. Mastery isn't merely about a perfect School Plan, a well-scheduled week, an improved registration process, or any of those back-office things. Mastery is found by going back to a simple question: Are the students doing better than they used to? That's why the principal should set targets.

He should follow up on those targets periodically by publishing data on everything from course grades to graduation rates to college admissions to average daily attendance to disciplinary referrals. Becoming a bit of a data junkie as a principal will feed your sense of mastery, even if the data reported isn't as good as you want it to be. Publishing data has a way of making it just a little more important, and merely publishing data will sometimes cause the staff to devise solutions to the challenges embedded in that data.

MOTIVATING STAFF

One of the principal's primary responsibilities, after attending to safety and order, is working with the staff to define, as unified a mission as possible, and to motivate them to achieve it. This is not easy in a high school that divides into so many curricular areas, but there are ways to do it. The principal's challenge is to work with the Leadership Team to identify goals toward which all staff can contribute. Hence, it's a good idea to establish goals that go across curricular areas, such as improving student attendance, reducing the proportion of "D" and "F" grades in each course, or reducing the number of disciplinary referrals.

No matter what someone teaches or does in a school, they can do something in their job to impact these kinds of goals, whether it is working on literacy strategies in their content area; establishing a safe, welcoming, and supportive environment; or improving student academic proficiency in one of the state-tested subjects. As teachers dig into the targets and their practices, they will discover that they really can impact student performance through their innovation.

In some settings, it may be difficult for the principal to unify the faculty around a singular sense of purpose, something that is particularly true in schools with a history of lower academic performance. However, there are still two other elements of the motivational triad (purpose, autonomy, mastery) available to him, so he should do his best to focus his energies on them. Even though staff may be reluctant to embrace school-wide goals, the principal will always find teachers who are interested in innovating. It may be that the best the principal can do in this situation is to support those innovators whose work will likely improve student learning. As teachers see their leading edge colleagues on the faculty begin various projects, other faculty will eventually join in, perhaps even bring the principal new ideas to improve the school.

MOTIVATING STUDENTS

Too often school principals fail to attend much to the motivation of the most important people in the building: the students. Although it is difficult to see just how the principal can impact student motivation, there are strategies that can make a difference. Let's start with purpose. The principal must never shy away from strategies that reinforce the primary purpose of the school: improving student achievement. Many schools implement school-wide systems to encourage students to deliver their best academic performance. Many secondary schools use the Renaissance model, a student-led, school-wide system that recognizes student achievement and improvement in GPAs. The principal must never pass up the opportunity to recognize students for their academic achievement. These recognitions should be for excellence as well as for improvement.

If we know anything about teenagers, it is this: they need enough space to develop their own autonomy. The classic teenager struggle is the quest for autonomy in a world that seeks to impose its conformity. Sadly, schools have a long history of doing things that promote conformity at an institutional level. Fortunately, advances in psychology as well as the growth of alternative learning environments and methods are slowly breaking down that wall of conformity behind which we have imprisoned so many kids.

To tap into student needs for autonomy, there are a number of things the principal and his staff can do. One curricular innovation that taps into this need for autonomy is Project-Based Learning, which affords students the opportunity to produce high-quality academic work in more meaningful and student-driven ways than before. Socratic seminars and discussion circles are also powerful strategies that put the student voice first. In English classes, teachers can let students self-select literature for the majority of their reading. The key to all these methods, though, is that teachers have to be willing to let students go where their interests take them, even if they occasionally follow less productive pathways.

In secondary schools, student leadership emerges as a more powerful force on the school climate if permitted, and it is in this area where the wise principal can also have an impact on student motivation. Kids want the space to try things out, and school has always been one of the very safest spaces for student expression and initiative to emerge. The principal, of course, is responsible for balancing this need for autonomy in students with the first responsibility for maintaining safety and order.

The principal is also faced with the challenge of navigating the political winds of his community in the area of student activities and initiative, which has often caused principals to say no to too many things. Over the years, the secondary principal will have the opportunity to say yes to all kinds of requests from student leaders, many of which they may not be able to pull off. Say yes wherever possible. What matters is not necessarily the success of a given event or activity; what matters is supporting the students' sense of initiative and ownership, even if the activity in question might not be very successful.

Another area where the principal can have an impact on students' sense of autonomy concerns school disciplinary policies. Overly restrictive disciplinary policies or enforcement can poison the atmosphere at school. If one doesn't exist, the school should form a discipline committee, which includes student representatives. The group should meet regularly and should be empowered to develop and pilot changes. What one discovers when a school tries out a change recommended by a discipline committee is that the world does not tilt off its axis, nor does Hell freeze over. Instead, the work of this group has the potential to eliminate or reduce sources of tension between students and staff. People adapt.

Speaking of disciplinary policies, we have entered an era where schools everywhere are striving to eliminate student suspension, to the maximum extent practicable. Many schools in California have eliminated suspension entirely. That's right: kids who fight, who lose their cool and say inappropriate things, who cheat, who lie, and even those who bully can remain in school. Garfield High School, located in an impoverished community in Los Angeles, has been a leader of this movement in California.

Jose Huerta, the school's courageous principal, was sick of seeing kids suspended because it was often the start of their pipeline out of school and into a life of worse things. So, he just ended suspensions one day. Instead of suspension, the school spent hours, days if needed, counseling kids who engaged in substantial misconduct. They made their parents come to school for conferences. They held conflict resolution meetings. Social workers addressed family and community issues to the extent possible. An on-campus community health clinic provided medical and dental care. The school became a place where compassionate services and care were wrapped around its at-risk students.

What Huerta understood was that his school needed to be a place where students had space to explore and develop their autonomy and where they did not live in a repressive school-to-prison-style environment. Attending to those affective needs made Huerta perhaps the greatest principal I have ever met in terms of his impact on a campus.

Kids need choices and chances if they are to thrive as learners and members of our community. They also need the opportunity to take charge of the assessment of their learning instead of our leaving assessment as something teachers do to them. Instead of excellence being some kind of secret that teachers keep from all but the most successful (conforming?) students, students in every class setting should see examples of what excellent papers, projects, lab reports, and performances look like *before* they produce their own.

If a teacher is teaching something new for which he has no model, then he should get one from a colleague or, even better, he should model the process himself as the students go through it. Kids want to do well, to achieve mastery, but they deserve to know what the target is, even if it remains out of reach for them at present. After all, mastery is an asymptote—right? And why not give the students a voice in the grading of their work, particularly their bigger projects and papers?

There is a wonderful strategy every school can employ that taps into student motivation and the development of their autonomy: student-led parent-teacher conferences. The idea behind the student-led conference is simple: return ownership and responsibility for learning to the student. Instead of a parent-teacher conference directed by the teacher where the student sits in silence, the student-led conference is conducted entirely by the student, following a template. The student prepares in advance for the conference, going through the self-assessment and reflection required by the template. He selects samples of his own work to support his findings about his progress.

On conference day, the student sits across from his parent, with the teacher at the end of the table, and it is the student who does the talking. The teacher's job is to be present and to ensure that the norms of the conference are adhered to. (Readers looking for more details about how to organize and conduct student-led conferences should consult the resources provided by Ashley Cronin through the Edutopia website.) These conferences have a remarkable effect on the students and their parents. Where school conferences have previously been about student weakness or misconduct, these conferences are about the students as developing learners. Implementing them on a school-wide basis can have a transformative effect.

CHAPTER 8 KEY POINTS AND STRATEGIES

1. After safety and order, the principal's primary responsibility is to attend to the motivation of everyone at school.
2. Carrots and sticks don't work to motivate employees or student learning. They never did. Remain focused on strategies to develop intrinsic motivation.
3. Man is in a constant search for a meaning and purpose to motivate him.
4. Man does not need a tensionless state; he needs to strive and struggle for a worthwhile goal.

5. Drive emerges from three factors: a clear sense of meaningful purpose, sufficient autonomy, and striving for mastery.
6. Support the innovators on your campus.
7. You are responsible for your own motivation as principal. Know your purpose.
8. Find ways to feed your own autonomy as principal.
9. You won't attain a sense of mastery as principal without determining what metrics matter most and periodically reporting them. The same is true for your staff.
10. Kids need autonomy to grow. Find ways to support it in your school.
11. Stop student suspension if you haven't done so already.
12. Insist that your teachers provide models of high-quality work to students in advance so that they know what excellence looks like.
13. Implement student-led conferences.

Nine

The Principal in Flow

A Master in the art of living draws no sharp distinction between his work and his play; his labor and his leisure; his mind and his body; his education and his recreation. He hardly knows which is which. He simply pursues his vision of excellence through whatever he is doing and leaves others to determine whether he is working or playing. To himself, he always appears to be doing both.
—François-Auguste-René de Chateaubriand

You give but little when you give of your possessions. It is when you give of yourself that you truly give.—Kahlil Gibran

Many who move from teaching into administration come to miss the flow experience of their best classroom days. They may particularly miss flow early in their careers while serving as assistant principals. The person who transitions into formal school-wide leadership still needs to be focused on flow: not necessarily her own sense of flow, but on helping others in the building achieve it.

As the principal digests this realization, her work will improve. She'll spend more time studying the best teachers in the school to see what conditions are in place that help them achieve those flow experiences. She'll talk with teachers more and more to *learn* from them, rather than to answer questions, solve their problems, or impart her own wisdom. She'll become less task oriented and more relationship oriented at school. She may even stop calling school "work" so much and start calling it "school" more often. After all, she is there to learn, too, and what she may learn is that the best organizations are those places that somehow foster drive and flow in greater numbers of people than lesser organizations.

The principal who embraces that worthy purpose of helping others experience flow at work begins to make the transition from being an administrator to being a leader.

IN MY EXPERIENCE
The Flow State

In the spring of 1980, I was a junior at UC Berkeley and also a member of the lightweight rowing team. On an otherwise typical spring morning, my second-boat colleagues and I dutifully rowed out to once again take our whupping from the better boat. We were an interesting boat, loaded with guys who, except for me, were small even for lightweight rowing. Some days we put up a decent fight, but most of the time we just got smoked.

On that fateful day, nothing special happened during the warm-up, the drills, or the practice pieces; we just did our work. Toward the end of practice, our coach told us to get a length in front of the first boat because we were going to run a practice race. The only question would be when the first boat passed us and by how much they would win after the 2,000-meter "race" was run. Once lined up, the coach called the start, and both boats were off. After 500 meters, to our surprise, we had not yet been caught by the first boat; in fact, we had maintained our starting advantage.

Surprised by our progress, we pressed on at 500 meters, hoping against hope that we might be able to hold on for longer than usual. And it was at about that point that something clicked in all nine of us aboard the boat, and we experienced something rowers call "swing": that rare moment where it all just comes together. I still don't know exactly what happened, but it felt like the boat lifted slightly out of the water. Everything sounded different than it ever had before.

At the end of each stroke, it seemed like we had an eternity of time to just relax, take a breath, and smoothly get up into the next stroke. The oars made one uniform, satisfying thump at the end of each stroke as we feathered the blades and prepared for the next stroke. As our oars caught the water at the start of each stroke, things went practically soundless. The boat moved faster and faster, but with less effort. The coxswain went completely silent, realizing that nothing needed to be said.

We lived together in that moment for the next four minutes until the 2,000 meters was completed. Not only had we all experienced swing together for the first time, we had increased our margin over the first boat throughout the piece, which had never occurred before—and would never occur again. By the time we got out of the boat, that swing experience had just gob smacked us into near-silence. Here we were, a bunch of self-described pencil-necks hanging on as second-stringers on a lightweight club crew, and yet we had clearly smoked our first boat, and it was easy, and joyful.

Over time, I discovered in my teaching career there were optimal days where that sense of swing—of flow—reappeared. In fact, it was at work where I was able to recapture flow most often. I put together lessons and units from time to time that were just transcendent, where my personal gifts (limited though they are) managed to mesh so seamlessly with the needs of my students that we all did better than we ever had before. Those were great times.

FLOW THEORY—MIHALY CSIKSZENTMIHALYI

While we all have those moments of optimal experience, like rowing with swing in the Oakland Estuary, it took a long time for psychology to adequately study flow and to provide us all with clues as to how we might create conditions that enable the flow state to occur more often and for more people. It was Mihaly Csikszentmihalyi (*me-high chick-sent-me-high-ee*) who did the primary research and theoretical development around flow, which is best described in his book *Flow: The Psychology of Optimal Experience* (1990).

During his work at the University of Chicago, Csikszentmihalyi became interested in what he first called optimal experience. To learn more about it, he recruited volunteers into a study in which they wore pagers that prompted them, at various times of day, to record in a journal what it was they were doing and how they were feeling. This simple strategy led to the development of a large body of data Csikszentmihalyi could mine for nuggets of optimal experience. He was then able to follow up his data with interviews of those participants in which they gave him and his researchers even more detail about what they were feeling during those optimal experiences. Many of his subjects used the word *flow* to describe their optimal experiences, and it stuck as the label for what Csikszentmihalyi was studying and defining. In rowing, we had swing; in life, we have flow. Here's how Csikszentmihalyi describes flow:

> It is what the sailor holding a tight course feels when the wind whips through her hair, when the boat lunges through the waves like a colt—sails, hull, wind, and sea humming a harmony that vibrates in the sailor's veins. It is what a painter feels when the colors on the canvas begin to set up a magnetic tension with each other, and a new thing, a living form, takes shape in front of the astonished creator. (1990, p. 3)

You can see at once that what Csikszentmihalyi's subjects revealed was that flow can happen in all kinds of settings. The information that emerged from his subjects was that they achieved flow frequently when the noise and distractions and difficulties of life, though still present, seemed to get filtered out by the mind. Just as Frankl taught us that man is only at his best when working in the service of a powerful purpose, so Csikszentmihalyi teaches us that flow frequently emerges during meaningful struggle:

> The best moments usually occur when a person's body or mind is stretched to its limits in a voluntary effort to accomplish something difficult and worthwhile. (1990, p. 3)

Over time, Csikszentmihalyi was able to learn from his subjects that the flow state most often occurred under the following eight conditions:

> First, the experience usually occurs when we confront tasks we have a chance of completing. Second, we must be able to concentrate on what we are doing. Third and fourth, the concentration is usually possible because the task undertaken has clear goals and provides immediate feedback. Fifth, one acts with a deep but effortless involvement that removes from awareness the worries and frustrations of everyday life. Sixth, enjoyable experiences allow people to exercise a sense of control over their actions. Seventh, concern for the self disappears, yet paradoxically the sense of self emerges stronger after the flow experience is over. Finally, the sense of the duration of time is altered; hours pass by in minutes, and minutes can stretch out to seem like hours. (1990, p. 49)

It's difficult to imagine that flow state occurring during a faculty meeting, right? But seriously, teachers, kids, and even administrators do experience the flow state while in school. And given that it is possible to achieve the flow state while at school doing one's job, shouldn't we consider doing what we can to nurture that?

ACHIEVING FLOW IN THE PRINCIPAL'S OFFICE

These are components that a principal needs to master if she is to be a successful principal:

1. getting and keeping the job of school principal;
2. managing the school's operations and routines effectively and efficiently;
3. devising and implementing a strategy for improving student achievement;
4. leading oneself and others to personal and professional growth that improves student achievement;
5. documenting the improvements in the school;
6. achieving flow in one's work; and
7. leading the school and departing from it in a manner that leaves it primed to keep on improving.

The sixth item, achieving flow, is the one that appears to be an outlier in this construct for success, but flow is essential to the life of the principal just as it is to the life of the teacher. By now it should surprise no one that being a school principal is hard. The days can be very long, probably too long, and unlike raising one's own children, the years never really seem to feel short. On its face, the daily job of the principal doesn't look like it meshes well with the eight conditions Csikszentmihalyi identified as components necessary for one to achieve the flow state. *But that depends on the person who is the principal, not the job itself.*

The principal has the power to decide how she responds to her circumstances at school, and those chosen responses have the power to impact the work of everyone else in the school. Consider the following summary (table 9.1), which compares a gimlet-eyed survivor principal with a successful principal across the eight domains underlying flow.

Our gimlet-eyed principal may end up a survivor in the system, but it's unlikely he'll ever enjoy the work. He may even attain most of the constructs of the successful principal over time. However, he'll most likely have few, if any, flow experiences on the job. His health will suffer. He will eventually be pushed into a desk at the district office, where he will coordinate grant funds until he hits retirement age.

Table 9.1. Two Principals and Their Relationship to Flow

Flow Occurs When . . .	The Gimlet-Eyed Principal Responds . . .	The Successful Principal Responds . . .
1. We confront tasks we have a chance of achieving	Seriously? NCLB? Common Core? You're kidding! We can never do it all.	Manage routines and procedures clearly. Stay focused on your goals.
2. One is able to concentrate	Not a chance. I'm always interrupted.	Efficiency and daily class visits minimize interruptions and make concentration possible.
3. The task has clear goals	Goals always change with the next election, the next boss.	The successful principal keeps herself and her staff focused on their goals.
4. The task provides immediate feedback	Only if it's a memo or report I have to finish before leaving.	Reports data continuously.
5. One experiences deep, effortless involvement	Seriously? I'm lucky to get 10 minutes at a time on anything.	Manages her health and wellness to achieve peak performance.
6. One engages in an enjoyable experience with a sense of control	I control almost nothing.	Defines what she can control and works on that.
7. Concern for self disappears in the moment	I'm always concerned for myself; I can be booted tomorrow.	Works for her students and staff, not the central office.
8. Time passes differently	Never fast enough. Never.	Happily puts in longer days when the work fulfills her purpose.

But a successful principal, who confronts the same challenges, expectations, and working conditions as her gimlet-eyed counterpart, is able to thrive and make a difference simply because she approaches her work with a different mind-set. She may be no more competent (indeed, she may be less so in a variety of areas) than our gimlet-eyed survivor, but the choices she makes and the attitude she brings with her to school each day changes those around her for the better.

PRINCIPAL SELF-CARE

Being the principal can be inimical to one's health and physical well-being. It becomes very difficult to take care of your health as a principal, especially if you have to drive more than a few minutes to and from school. It is kind of odd that principals often work in buildings with great workout facilities, including weight rooms, pools, and running tracks, yet are seldom able to actually use them. Some principals will make sporadic use of their school's fitness facilities, but most don't. To avoid working herself into an early grave, the principal must find a way to get some exercise. For many, the only solution one can consistently implement is to get up early and get it done first thing in the morning. Whatever your preferred workout is, the best time to do it consistently—if you're a principal—is before you put on your school clothes.

The second element of self-care for the principal is diet. Here again, the way school is organized can make eating well a real challenge. The healthiest principals all make a common decision: they prepare their own healthy lunch and bring it to school with them. Those principals who consistently eat from the school's cafeteria or nearby restaurants often end up less healthy than their lunch-bag-toting colleagues.

For high school principals, a further dietary challenge arises: banquet seasons. High school principals attend a spate of banquets every winter and spring; it's a natural element of the arc of the school year, and it can be a killer to one's diet. The healthiest principals manage to do banquet season without gaining weight. They request the vegetarian option. They decline dessert. They drink no soft drinks, sticking to tea and water. It does require some self-discipline to make these kinds of choices, but principals in search of their own flow state have a more powerful motive for making them than survival-oriented principals. Who do you want to be?

PROFESSIONAL LEARNING AND ENGAGEMENT

The happiest and most effective principals find ways to be more professionally engaged and actively learning than their survivor colleagues.

They join their professional associations. They volunteer their time to them, serve as officers, and even become legislative advocates. The successful principal faithfully follows Steven Covey's (2004) mantra to sharpen the saw in order to improve efficiency. It does seem a paradox that time the principal spends away from the building professionally engaged actually makes her stronger, wiser, and more effective. But it does.

Some school districts and superintendents support principal engagement in local community organizations, such as Rotary or Kiwanis clubs. Another way the principal can sharpen the saw is by returning to the classroom—to teach. This doesn't necessarily mean teaching an ongoing class in one's school, although that can be very rewarding. Instead, some successful principals often end up involved teaching at the university level.

What the successful principal knows is that she learns a great deal by teaching. It forces her to read literature most likely written since her own graduate degree was earned. She confronts the same challenge as her own faculty each and every week: figuring out how to get the best performance out of her students and herself. She'll also learn a great deal from her students if she is open to it. Teaching in a college setting causes the successful principal to digest and process what she's learning in her own career and find ways to use that to enrich the lives of her college students.

YOUR TIME

When the school day ends, go home. This is difficult in secondary schools, but still doable most days of the week if the principal deploys all her administrators properly. Once after-school supervision is handled, why stick around? There are no great curricular or instructional improvements to be made by staying late in the building. If you're regularly working into the evening, you either have an efficiency problem, a control problem, or a systems problem that needs to be addressed.

The best solution to the overflowing inbox is often simple: get up, pack, and go home. The logic is evident: you're no good to your staff if you work yourself to exhaustion or if you neglect your family or personal needs by staying in the office too much. Being the principal doesn't end right at 3:00 p.m., but when the supervisory need to be in the building is done for the day, then it is time to leave and go do whatever it is that rejuvenates you. For the successful principal, that might mean going to the university to teach, or going home to join her family, to be there when her children play, compete, or just do their homework. Being a successful principal simply must not be inimical to being successful in life.

What the successful principal discovers over time is that all her choices, including exercising early, going home, and becoming more professionally engaged, truly do alter the manner in which time passes, which is a part of the flow state. It is an oft-repeated paradox: if you want to get something done on time, you should ask a busy person to do it. That paradox is always in play for our successful principal. Because she is busy, engaged, learning, healthy, and motivated by her goals, she just gets things done. She may not necessarily get more things done than our gimlet-eyed survivor, but she learns to get the *right* things done and, better still, she very often has enthusiastic people in her building who want to take on projects that improve the school. Thus, she further reaps the benefits of that old saying about many hands making the work light.

This is when something called the flywheel effect kicks in. The *flywheel effect* is the term given to describe the phenomenon of the steadily increasing ease with which one can somehow do more work. Richard DuFour spoke and wrote about the flywheel effect that ensues in schools that successfully build high-functioning Professional Learning Communities. At first, a flywheel (think of a heavy, weighted wheel or gear) is difficult to turn. An object at rest tends to stay at rest, and its weight makes starting up its motion difficult. But once a flywheel starts turning, its weight makes it more difficult to slow it down, and, in a nice benefit, increasing its speed requires much less effort than was needed to get it started in the first place.

That same flywheel effect can happen on a larger scale at school, and when it happens, it's beautiful. The successful principal in search of the flow state at work, both for herself and her staff, has to manage herself and her time and her engagement with her own personal needs in mind. It does go against our country's traditional Protestant work ethic to just pack up and leave the building, but it's essential to do just that if you and your staff are going to thrive and attain flow.

WHAT THE PRINCIPAL CAN CONTROL

The sixth domain underlying the flow state is that the person is engaged in an enjoyable activity over which she has some control. Teachers have a great deal of control over their lessons, assessments, and instructional strategies. Teachers still control their time, and their noninstructional time is further protected by their contracts. The principal, on the other hand, lacks that same level of built-in autonomy in the work, which can be frustrating at times. She may find herself buffeted with responsibilities and initiatives hatched by the central office that simply must be implemented.

Even so, the principal, through her choices, often can control more things than she realizes. The most important thing she controls, of course, is her own attitude. No matter what is thrown her way, she can control how she responds. That self-control over her attitude is the single biggest tool she has at her disposal. Beyond basic self-control, though, there are many other things a principal can control if she chooses. Here are a few:

1. The principal controls the site meeting calendar. She also has the leadership potential to make sure that all meetings are purposeful, kind, and supportive.
2. The principal can steer a school's conversation and initiatives in support of data points she chooses. If she wants to work on attendance, then she can do it. If she is concerned about student conduct, then she can focus on disciplinary referrals. There is one proviso here: she should not pick too many data areas for extended focus because the school can lose focus. Three is a good maximum.
3. The principal can control the degree to which she delegates leadership and projects to others. Very few things actually have to be done from start to finish by the principal herself.
4. The principal also has the prerogative to select those on her staff to whom she delegates leadership and projects. Exercising these choices with wisdom and intention can grow the capacity of the staff.
5. The principal has the power to control certain points of emphasis in a school's classrooms. Some schools choose to focus on the use of AVID (Advancement Via Individual Determination) strategies. Others will focus on project-based learning. Whatever strategy is selected, promoting school-wide use of it can have a powerful effect.
6. The principal can sometimes control or move the direction of community conversation and involvement. Some principals reap great benefits for their schools through fundraising. Others build strong, supportive parent engagement systems, which can have a clear impact on their school.
7. The principal controls the customer service ethic of the school's support staff. We don't usually pay enough attention to this critical domain of school leadership.
8. The principal herself, through her daily interactions with everyone, exercises the most powerful impact on what it feels like to be at her school.

These areas all give the principal the opportunity to work with intention, to select and refine directions. You'll notice that many of these choices give the principal the opportunity to impact what her school *feels* like. What school feels like, how people characterize it in emotional terms, affects just how much people enjoy being there. An emotionally healthy and happy environment where all strive for growth is the successful principal's secret sauce. Since that secret sauce is so difficult to measure, the central office is unlikely to prescribe what the principal should do in service of that need—which means she has a lot of freedom to exercise her creative energy (and that of the staff) to make her school a better place for growth. That's a great privilege, and it provides the principal with a great way to distinguish herself as a leader.

STRATEGIES FOR HELPING STAFF ACHIEVE FLOW

Once the principal has taken care of her own needs, she is better able to make choices that support the flow-state needs of everyone else on her staff. She likely has developed a better understanding of those conditions that make her work more enjoyable, meaningful, and productive, and this same understanding can be applied to the choices and initiatives she undertakes to improve the school itself. It can be helpful to think of all the domains of the flow state Csikszentmihalyi identifies because each of those eight areas gives the principal something to consider in her leadership. While the principal may not need to take specific actions to impact each of the eight domains, it is worthwhile to periodically ponder how the principal's choices may be impacting those domains. Table 9.2 gives a brief synopsis of how the principal can impact the domains of the flow state.

While table 9.2 is certainly not a strategic planning tool, it is a worthwhile lens through which to view the principal's leadership choices. A useful exercise for a Leadership Team to go through might start by listing what presently exists in support of each of the domains, and then generating and discussing ideas that might be useful to support improvement in the domains that need it. This is a much different way for a Leadership Team to do its work than is the norm in schools, and it certainly has its risks. At a minimum, the principal hoping to move in this direction would want to build some background knowledge in advance of this exercise.

After building background about the idea of optimal experience and flow, one place to begin would be for the team members to describe their own flow experiences while teaching. As those experiences are shared, and as the team discusses them, the principal's overarching question might be this: What can we do together to increase opportunities for all our staff to have more teaching moments in flow? This question doesn't ask for a new technique or initiative or specific instructional strategy; rather, it asks everyone to look at the domains of flow and to imagine what can be done to better support those domains.

Table 9.2. How the Principal Can Impact the Eight Domains of the Flow State

Flow Occurs When . . .	What the Principal Can Do for Her Staff
1. We confront tasks we have a chance of achieving	Give staff some freedom to define reasonable improvement goals in student performance.
2. One is able to concentrate	Time! Don't take up teacher time during conference periods. Respect teachers' needs for time to reflect, refresh, and rejuvenate. Sub for your teachers on occasion.
3. The task has clear goals	This is where a principal's wisdom and guidance can be essential. Help your teachers create specific, measurable goals.
4. The task provides immediate feedback	Think of the word *immediate* as meaning within a few weeks or, perhaps, up to one quarter of a school year.
5. One experiences deep, effortless involvement	This comes when teachers get to play to their strengths in terms of instructional strategies. Allow them enough choice to use their best strategies.
6. One engages in an enjoyable experience with a sense of control	Providing teachers choices over methods as well as specific areas of learning will enhance teachers' sense of control.
7. Concern for self disappears in the moment	This is a natural by-product of successful teaching, which plays to a teacher's strengths. Sometimes that means the principal needs to trust the teacher's instincts just a little more.
8. Time passes differently	Time will pass differently for both teachers and students when they are actively engaged in meaningful learning in which all students are successful.

One benefit of this approach is that many of the strategies the team is likely to come up with *are entirely within the school's control*. No new funding is required. No one has to amend the School Plan. There's no need to build community support. The kind of work that is likely to support the flow state among faculty is about the learning environment, working conditions, and trust. It's about relationships, not new tasks. Face it: there are already plenty of tasks; just read a Single Plan for Student Achievement here in California if you're not sure schools are doing enough. Focusing on the eight domains of the flow state, even a little, would be a great way to work on relationships, which schools don't always do very well.

A school that intentionally focuses on strategies to support flow experiences among its faculty is going to be an exciting, engaging place for staff and students. Instead of focusing on difficulties, such a school will face things with a growth mind-set. Instead of bemoaning poor performance, the principal in such a school will first look to herself and her site Leadership Team, seeking to understand what they can do as leaders to better support, empower, and equip teachers so that they are more likely to deliver their best work. In such a school, teachers will happily share their flow experiences with their colleagues so that everyone can grow from them and figure out how to recreate the flow experience across more classrooms. And obviously, in such a school, all children will be far more likely to achieve their learning potential.

A PRINCIPAL'S EXPERIENCES IN FLOW

Now let's get back to a successful principal. Obviously, attending to the needs of students and staff is her primary responsibility, but in doing so, one would hope that she gets to have her own flow experiences as well. Being the principal is a little like being a parent on an airplane when the oxygen masks drop from the ceiling: even though our instincts tell us to take care of our children first, adult passengers are instructed to first secure their own oxygen masks before they assist their children. (And let's not imagine the school as an airplane potentially going down—please!) Once the new principal has established order, gone through her entry plan, done what she can in terms of her self-care, and empowered and supported her staff to take ownership of the school's improvement, what kinds of moments and days can she hope to have that will bring her the pleasures and learning experiences of flow?

Flow experiences can occur for the principal all over school and at various times of day, but they may differ somewhat from the pure flow-state experiences Csikszentmihalyi describes in his work. Flow experiences for the principal may have limited time spans and occur after a lot of groundwork. For the principal, the flow state may often be something she experiences as she observes the work of her students and staff, including

- Eureka moments when a teaching team implements a strategy they have designed and implemented together in order to address an ongoing challenge;
- observing teachers engaged in a successful lesson study;
- experiencing large, positive community turnout for an event;
- observing the evident pride and cognitive growth through student exhibitions;
- being present for a college admissions celebration.

IN MY EXPERIENCE
Flow in the Principal's Office

Flow experiences can occur for the principal all over school and at various times of day. My own flow experiences had limited time spans but often occurred after a lot of groundwork. When I think back on my own flow experiences as a principal, I most vividly recall these:

1. My team of biology teachers launched a four-day intervention and enrichment session they labeled "interrichment," which required hundreds of kids to literally go to different classrooms during their biology class period and either get re-taught the skills they needed to be proficient or, if proficient, engage in an enrichment lesson. On the appointed day, the teachers sent hundreds of kids to new classrooms where they engaged in the lesson they needed. It went flawlessly. Kids were elated at getting a second chance to learn something—and to replace a low test score. Teachers exercised their creativity and wisdom to contrive alternate methods for teaching the material the students hadn't yet learned well enough. Meanwhile, students who had learned the material weren't held back by their peers who just needed a second chance or an alternate teaching strategy; they got to do something extra. Every teacher and every student I saw was actively, positively engaged. I'll always remember one boy—a really struggling student who became successful in science through this process—racing over to me one day during enrichment and opening his hand to reveal the rat brain he had just excised during the enrichment dissection he was doing. Those were incredible days for me because my dreams for my students and my staff were all coming true.
2. During morning professional development meetings in the spring, teachers were divided into interdisciplinary teams where they first participated in Learning Walks together, focused on observing strategies that would promote literacy. Over the next few weeks, they intentionally planned lessons making use of strategies they were learning through their professional development, using a modified Lesson Study process. They conducted those lessons and then reported on them and their results a few weeks later. I was never so proud of this faculty as I was that morning. They were so engaged as learners and colleagues. The professional practice of every teacher was improved.
3. Our social science department conceived of a year-long focus on the issue of immigration as a lens through which all of the department's courses could periodically be brought together into a project-based learning activity. The kids wrote research papers in small groups over

(continued)

the fall, and in the spring they developed PowerPoint presentations in which they had to take a position on an immigration issue and propose initiatives to address the problem. Late in the spring, they held large-scale seminars in our theater, inviting prominent guests to engage with them on the issue. Guests included a sitting member of the United States Congress, a local mayor, university professors, and community activists. It was the most effective social science experience I ever saw implemented in my career. Being present during those seminars in our theater was a highlight of my career as principal in that school.

4. Our high school's annual celebration of our diverse cultures culminated on a Friday evening in February with a series of performances in our gymnasium for which we charged a small fee that offset the costs the student body accrued. This event involved hundreds of students in the school in completely independent rehearsals of dance performances and songs for weeks. That Friday evening event in our gym was the only time each year the gym was full for an evening event. I'll never forget our Polynesian dance troupe's performance of a traditional (for Polynesia) fundraising dance where parents are encouraged to get out of their seats during the performance and actually join the kids on the floor—while donating cash. One parent in particular will forever stick in my mind. He was as destitute as you can possibly imagine. We had met in my office twice because of issues with his child. He was in terrible health, and his son was a mess, but to see the joy on his face as he hobbled out on that gym floor (he could hardly walk) to dance with his son and his friends was one of the most moving experiences of my career. One only understands these things through personal engagement with kids and their families, and I was blessed to have made enough time for that.

5. Every November a small group of teachers would volunteer their after-school time to help seniors write their college entrance essays. Our students really struggled with this task because most of them had learned English as their second language. One afternoon, our top student, Mai-Lin, sat down next to me at my table for my help with her essay. Despite being a superb learner, she was a wreck and, thanks to my superb counseling skills, soon ended up in tears. Her father had died when she was little, and her mother was presently fighting cancer. Mai-Lin was a mess for days as she struggled with her essay, but we slowly got through it, and she achieved her goal of submitting something meaningful. A few weeks later, I met her mother during a parent learning walk through our school, and I was blessed with her gratitude at having helped her daughter through this challenge. Tears all the way around, for all three of us. And a few weeks later, Mai-Lin brought me her acceptance letter from Harvard, becoming just one of two students in my career who would enter Harvard. As I write today, Mai-Lin is a thriving student who attends Harvard on full scholarship.

> While each of these five experiences do not perfectly fit into Csikszentmihalyi's conception of the flow state, these were peak experiences for me. They occurred because the people who worked in my schools were empowered to take on big challenges knowing that I had their back. They occurred because I found ways to build trusting relationships with teachers willing to take risks. As teachers took on more responsibility and ownership, I was freed up to spend more time watching, applauding, supporting, or just sitting with kids as they struggled with their college entrance essays. As the flywheel picked up speed and we did more, we got better at many things and it became easier to improve than it had before. On each of these days, and many more over my career, I drove home knowing that our collective improvement as a school was changing the arc of the lives of our students, and there is no better feeling.

CHAPTER 9 KEY POINTS AND STRATEGIES

1. Everyone can have flow experiences while at work in school.
2. The principal is responsible for nurturing the conditions that lead to flow experiences in school.
3. Flow emerges as a result of struggle. It occurs when people are striving.
4. The principal can support flow experiences in her school by viewing her work through the lens of the eight domains of flow.
5. Principal self-care is a crucial area, necessary to help all others in her school have flow experiences.
6. Sharpen the saw. The successful principal takes care of her own needs first.
7. When the school day ends, the successful principal goes home.
8. The successful principal leads in such a way that the school reaps the benefits of the flywheel effect.
9. The principal's attitude is powerful and entirely within her control, which is why she must do all she can to keep it positive.
10. The successful principal remains focused on what she can control.
11. An emotionally happy and healthy environment, where all strive for growth, is the successful principal's secret sauce.
12. Flow experiences for the successful principal often occur only after a great deal of groundwork.

Ten

The Departing Principal

Ever has it been that love knows not its own depth until the hour of separation.—Kahlil Gibran

Work is love made visible. And if you cannot work with love but only with distaste, it is better that you should leave your work and sit at the gate of the temple and take alms of those who work with joy.—Kahlil Gibran

This is the true joy in life, the being used for a purpose recognized by yourself as a mighty one; the being thoroughly worn out before you are thrown on the scrap heap; the being a force of nature instead of a feverish selfish little clod of ailments and grievances complaining that the world will not devote itself to making you happy.—George Bernard Shaw

The principal's tenure in a school does not always come to an ordinary conclusion. Over the course of a career in schools, I saw quite a few principal departures, several of which were quite notable:

- A principal at one of the highest achieving schools in California, who was happy in her job and had the respect of the staff and community, was summarily transferred to another school in our district to serve as their principal. A few months later she happily accepted a much higher-paying position as a principal elsewhere in our county, not wishing to work any longer for the school district that had moved her just because it could.
- A powerful and successful principal was pushed into a made-up position at the district office one spring, primarily as a result of whispers about his relationship with a teacher on the staff. He left the district that spring, moving to another part of the state.
- Two extremely successful and powerful principals who led high schools with a strong rivalry were flip-flopped to one another's schools. It was a naked power play that left two schools with principals who didn't want to lead their new schools.

- A new principal, recently divorced and relocated from another county and new to her position, happily informed her superintendent of her blossoming romantic relationship with a teacher on the staff. She was immediately moved to an office in the Adult Education program immediately, her career path devastated.
- A successful principal, recently honored as his county's principal of the year, lost his position when the school's student council held a themed dress-up day that was insensitive to the school's Latino population.

These stories, and so many more, point out just how tenuous the principal's hold on his position is. Lest we forget, no one can be removed from his position more quickly than the principal; it can happen in an instant. Because it is so easy to be removed as a principal, wizened hands in the principal's office learn that it's a good strategy not to stand out—at all. Principals who garner a lot of attention for themselves, intentionally or not, often end up as targets by small-minded board members and central office administrators. Board members are politicians, and central office administrators are political appointees. In many communities, attention directed to a successful principal ends up being perceived by some of these folks as attention directed away from them and their own leadership. The Machiavellians in those positions, and there are many, have some brutal tools at their disposal, and they will be exercised.

Given that a principal's tenure is always subject to a sudden end, what should he do? While the temptation in this situation is to lead in a manner that ruffles no feathers and to follow a passive, managerial course of action, it's still better to have led a school in a manner that changes people's lives for the better than to merely manage it and attain ordinary results. Taking that stance for transformational leadership and living it out in daily practice means that the principal is likely to stand out at some point and become a target for promotion or otherwise. The successful principal is one who does his job with integrity, leaves his school better than he found it, and ensures that it will continue to improve. The successful principal should be thoughtful about his departure on two levels: the personal and the professional, and he should spend some time contemplating his strategies in this area, unpleasant though it may be.

PREPARING FOR DEPARTURE: THE PERSONAL DIMENSION

As we saw in the previous chapter, the successful principal takes care of himself first so that he can give to others. In the context of preparing for departure, that means that even though departure may not come precisely at a time of his own choosing, the successful principal is prepared to cope with it and to help the staff cope with it. The staff will need care once it gets out that a successful principal is leaving; teachers don't like breaking in new principals, particularly when a visible, successful principal is leaving.

The first thing every principal needs to take a hard look at is money: his own personal finances. This always seems to be a subject not discussed in school leadership, but it is an important issue that should not be ignored. It's a bad idea for a principal to take on long-term expenses that require the same salary stream to fund over several years. Bigger mortgages, car payments, boat payments, or second homes are generally beyond the carrying capacity of teachers, which means that it's risky for a principal to take on those kinds of obligations since he could very well end up a classroom teacher again in a matter of moments.

When it becomes evident that a principal has to leave a school, that struggle is much easier to manage if he has not changed his material lifestyle much since becoming a principal. It's wise for a principal to continue living in the same house in which he resided while working as a teacher. Avoid additional debt. That financial positioning provides a sense of security—even power—that can make it easier to weather the difficult times if they should come.

Related to the issue of money is another thing we don't talk about much: readiness to retire. In California, a schoolteacher or administrator can retire and start collecting a pension as early as age 55. Our State Teachers Retirement System (CalSTRS) urges teachers and administrators to meet with CalSTRS representatives when they are relatively young—in their 40s—in order to develop a clear picture of what their financial future will be like when they retire. It is surprising to see just how few do this. Wouldn't you want to be prepared for your financial future? The wise administrator knows his numbers and what his retirement benefit will look like years before he must seriously consider retirement. Knowing his numbers well enables a principal to plan for an early retirement—if desired—and, most important, to maintain control and comfort over the direction his life may take. That's a great gift.

A second aspect of the personal preparation for leaving a school principal position is networking. Many struggle with this because networking is *work*; that's why *work* is in its name. Networking requires introverted administrators to step out of their introversion and take some risks. Here in Southern California, the best way to be part of a network of school administrators is to join the Association of California School Administrators (ACSA), our state's association for school administrators. ACSA hosts many events, from local dinners, to mixers, to conferences.

ACSA also hosts advanced training and development opportunities. Teaching at the university level can help a principal expand his network and reputation. The other thing that can expand the principal's network is his weekly Friday letter. In addition to sending it to his staff, district staff, and the community, there are many friends and acquaintances to whom he should send the letter each week, just as a way of keeping in touch.

An important element of being prepared for departure from a principal position is to have personal papers at the ready. Sometimes a promotional opportunity too good to pass up will rise quickly. At other times, a successful principal will get that fateful tap on the shoulder about an opportunity he never conceived of. And, of course, sometimes the district will change course and want a new leader in a school. Each of these situations means that the successful principal must always be prepared with a current resume, current letters of recommendation, and the readiness to reenter a competitive selection process.

In the private sector, this kind of mind-set and preparation is routine, but that is not the case in school administration. Many outstanding school administrators choose to remain in positions where they are less than completely happy in large part because they don't want to reenter the competitive job application process. While it is difficult and frustrating to put yourself out there on the job market, it can be more difficult to go to work every day less than satisfied with how your organization is treating you.

The most important element of being prepared for departure from service as a school principal is the successful principal's family and friends. The principal will need their support, whether it's because he is taking on the challenges of a promotional opportunity, leading a school in a new configuration, or facing the possibility of being pushed out of the principal's office. Not all principals share their work life in much detail with their loved ones, which can be a mistake.

Being the principal is a bit like being the pastor in a neighborhood church: it's a calling, not just a job. It both exhausts and exhilarates, and it takes a toll on family and friends. If you don't tell your loved ones what you're going through, then how can you expect them to be sympathetic and supportive when you have to go through a transition? It's not heroic to keep your struggles at work a personal secret from those closest to you, even if you were raised to believe that being closemouthed about difficulties at work was the right way to behave.

A corollary of sharing your situation with your loved ones is this: don't whine to anyone else! Seriously, everyone has troubles. No one in your school wants to hear about your troubles. Complaining about things only has a way of biting a successful principal in the behind later on. Even in Southern California where there are hundreds of schools, educational leadership is a small world, and the last thing the successful principal needs is to develop a reputation for whining or not supporting his district.

Sometimes the end of a successful principal's time in a school is hard. But whining about it to others or buying into any pity parties is simply not in the principal's best interest nor, most important, in the school's best interest. The principal is a public servant to his school and its community until the day he packs his belongings and marches out the door. It is important to be a grown-up and to model steadfast character in the best possible way. It isn't always easy, but it is right.

PREPARING FOR DEPARTURE: THE PROFESSIONAL DIMENSION

Given just how essential the school principal is to every measure of success in a school, you'd think that school districts would invest time and thought in succession planning, but they seldom do. Some school districts try to identify and support aspiring administrators through in-house academies, but those academies mostly prepare teachers who are aspiring to introductory administrative work. Most school districts, as a matter of policy, run open recruitments for all principal positions. As a result, a new principal in a school could come from anywhere, which makes succession planning, as it's done in the business world, nearly impossible. So, the successful principal who cares deeply about his school will run into the challenge of how to ensure that the work he and his Leadership Team have done over the years continues after his departure.

The very best principals create a legacy at the schools they serve. If they have done their work well, involved all staff to their potential, and maintained a safe, happy, and orderly environment, then the school will continue to operate in much the same manner long beyond the principal's time of service. Doing the work of motivating staff and helping them all develop their niches as leaders is the very best way to prepare a school for the principal's departure, even a sudden departure. This is why distributing leadership across the campus, especially to teacher-leaders in their Professional Learning Communities, is the surest way to leave a legacy as a principal. While it's true that a new principal can come in and make many changes to existing structures, it is usually unwise, especially if a school is functioning well. No principal anywhere wants a one-and-done tag hung on their resume, which is usually what happens when they try to make first-year changes in a school previously led by a successful principal.

Another key element of preparing professionally for departure is the preparation of assistant principals, which is especially applicable in secondary schools. During a leadership transition, districts will almost always try to keep an assistant principal or two in place at the school in order to ensure continuity. This is especially true if the school has been functioning well. So, the more responsibility the principal delegates to his co-administrators, the more likely it is that the school will open smoothly and function well when the new principal takes his place. During those final weeks or months before departure, the successful principal should be driven more than ever by a simple maxim: don't do anything for the staff that they can do for themselves (see Schmidt, 2002). This course of action is not a case of being lazy or coasting to the finish line; it's preparing the staff for taking on more responsibility.

THE NUTS AND BOLTS OF DEPARTURE

When it's time for a successful principal to depart from a school, it's important that he be thoughtful and strategic about it. If he is being pushed out by the school board or the district's leadership, his departure announcement requires care. If at all possible, the principal should reach agreement with the superintendent about the timing and manner of his departure announcement. Because the departure of a principal can be traumatic, its announcement must be planned with the best interests of the school in mind. Whether it's better to wait or to announce quickly, it's critical that the principal be in concert with the district-level leadership. This is not the time for whining or complaining; it's a time to demonstrate character and professionalism.

If the principal is departing of his own accord—for promotion, retirement, or a new career direction—it remains critical for him to announce his departure after consulting with his district leadership. After all, there is still a school to run. The announcement itself should be made first to the faculty in a meeting. If possible, a district official should attend who can speak about the district's plans for the selection process for the successor principal. The announcement itself should be clear, short, and positive. The announcement should be followed up with a written document, possibly the principal's weekly letter. My own Friday letter where I announced my retirement can be found in textbox 10.1.

The early announcement of a departure can be beneficial for a school for a number of reasons. First, an early announcement gives people time to process it. Announcing early means that your district is free to begin the recruitment and selection of a replacement earlier than is the norm, and that gives the staff a better opportunity to participate in that process. It is important that their voices be heard and that they develop a relationship with the successor principal as early as possible. The long time period also gives the staff more time to assume greater ownership of the school's daily operations. In his final months, the departing principal should work hard at not doing for the staff things they are able to do for themselves. A departure done right means that the faculty will keep on working to improve its professional practice under the leadership of those with the most skin in the game: themselves.

IN MY EXPERIENCE
Saying Farewell

To: The Magnolia Staff and Community
From: Robert Cunard
January 8, 2016

THE FRIDAY LETTER

Quotes of the Week

"Twenty years from now you will be more disappointed by the things you didn't do than by the ones you did do. So throw off the bowlines. Sail away from the safe harbor. Catch the trade winds in your sails. Explore. Dream. Discover."—Mark Twain

"If people concentrated on the really important things in life, there'd be a shortage of fishing poles."—Doug Larson

"Half our life is spent trying to find something to do with the time we have rushed through life trying to save."—Will Rogers, Autobiography, 1949

"When a man retires, his wife gets twice the husband but only half the income."—Chi Chi Rodriguez

Earlier this week I met with our superintendent and submitted my notice of retirement, effective June 30, 2016. My decision is the result of a mix of personal and professional reasons, and today I share those with you.

If you look around Orange County, you'll discover that there are 68 comprehensive public high schools, which means that just 68 men and women in our county of over three million people have the same job as me. Of the 68, just four are older than I am. One of the principals was my student at Irvine High in 1993. Although I'm only 56 and relatively healthy, it takes a certain amount of endurance and tenacity to be the principal, and the job can wear you out. Some things do get easier with the accumulated wisdom of age, but only some things. The inbox still never sleeps. If the cell phone rings, you have to answer it, no matter what the circumstances. I still spend about 100 nights a year eating dinner out as a result of being the principal. This has taken a toll on my overall health, and if I don't stop and get off this train for a while, the long-term consequences I see down the road don't look very good. So one of the very first reasons behind this decision is that I need to stop, breathe, and change my own life.

(continued)

A feature of being a principal is that there is no way to do it less—or to do less of it. You either drink from the fire hose or you don't drink at all. There is no such thing as part time, or reduced workload. There is no emeritus status. I'd love to start my days rowing or surfing and then come in to work; I have friends who do just that every day before going in to their jobs. But that's not possible in this job. Showing up at 9:00 a.m. when your school comes to life two hours earlier is simply not going to cut it. What kind of example does that set? Our kids and our staff and our community deserve a principal who is 100 percent committed, and that means showing up early and, frequently, staying late.

I've also spent a lot of time thinking about what is best for Magnolia, and that has been a big factor in this decision. I've had the privilege of serving as our principal for six school years, which is about as a long a run as a principal ever gets. For context, consider that of the 20 principals currently serving in AUHSD, only one besides me has been at the same school for six years. During those six years we've done some great things together here at Magnolia. The senior class of 2016 will smash all records for college admission and A–G completion rates. We are improving our community engagement. We have, for the most part, successfully transitioned to teaching the Common Core State Standards. This fall we made it through a major administrative transition, Federal Program Monitoring, and a successful WASC mid-cycle visit. It was difficult and stressful at times, but I'm glad I was here for it. Magnolia's next principal inherits a different school than the one I found back in 2010, and that lucky soul will enter with time to get to know all of you, our kids, and our programs without the added pressure of a near-term WASC or other bureaucratic challenges. It's a good time for a transition.

My own personal transition will probably be a little more awkward than the one the school will go through. I don't have a whole list of amazing plans. I don't have another job to go to. I do intend to surf and row and read on my own schedule for the first time ever. Kristen will continue to work for several years, which means I'll become our primary cook, grocery shopper, and all-around domestic worker. I'll continue to teach some college courses and do some school accreditations. I won't be writing Friday Letters to you anymore, but I do have ideas about some things I want to write. I suppose there is a chance that I could return to work in a school system in some capacity later on; I'll just have to wait and see what emerges.

Back in the fall of 1980, I was a senior at UC Berkeley and needed a way to get one credit so that I could avoid an additional class during the rowing season. I was preparing to take the Law School Admissions Test and to apply to Law School. I earned that credit by volunteering twice a week in an elementary school in inner-city Richmond, 10 miles to the north. I had the time and a car, so that's what I did, getting placed in a third grade classroom where I inherited the slow reading group for that fall and winter. The third time I came to read with the kids, a little African American girl bounced out of her seat,

> *raced over to our table in the corner, and pulled her chair right next to mine as we got ready to read. I will never forget the look in her eyes as she snugged up as close as she could that morning; it was special and it was life-changing for me. That little girl's face made me a teacher and, more important, a better man than I ever would have been had I gone into law. Who knew that being a teacher (15 years), coach (5 years), activities director (4 years), assistant principal (9 years), and principal (10 years) could be so satisfying and rewarding?*
>
> *I send you this letter today with gratitude for our having been together these past six years. Magnolia has made me a better person. I think I was the right principal for our school, but that judgment will be made by others over time. During this final semester here with you, I'll still be pretty busy. We need to achieve consensus around our advisement program. We're doing some important work of our own around our vision, and I want to see us succeed in that. I'm doing a WASC visit to another high school this spring. I'll also teach another school leadership course this spring to graduate students. But my most important work will still be the daily work of being our principal. It's the very best job I've ever had, and I'm so proud to have been a part of our school.*

THE LEGACY OF THE SUCCESSFUL PRINCIPAL

The successful principal usually loves his work, his school, and the school's community. Being successful requires that kind of love and commitment. And while most principals do the work with little expectation of recognition or reward beyond the paycheck, the successful principal discovers that he is loved and is missed. Once news of the principal's departure is public, he should be prepared for the reactions of the students, many who may be quite candid. The students are the most important element of the successful principal's legacy. If the departing principal has been successful, the students now attend a school that is better than when he found it. The successful principal has the satisfaction of knowing the stories of his graduates now in college because the way he ran their school expanded and empowered their dreams. For the successful principal, the success of his students and others who will follow them is what being a principal is all about.

CHAPTER 10 KEY POINTS AND STRATEGIES

1. You may not be in charge of the timing or circumstances of your departure as principal. Be prepared.
2. Principals lose their jobs over political fallout all the time.

3. Despite the risks, it's better to lead a school with transformative purpose and passion than it is to manage toward the middle.
4. Pay attention to personal finance. Live like a teacher; you may be one again sooner than you think.
5. Be prepared for and knowledgeable about your retirement income and options at an early age.
6. Network, even if you hate it.
7. Be at the ready when it comes to personal papers. You never know what opportunity or situation may come your way at a moment's notice.
8. No whining—especially at work. You're the principal; be steadfast.
9. Secure a legacy by distributing leadership for school improvement to many people in the school.
10. Be purposeful and thoughtful about announcing your departure.

References

Barth, R. S. (1990). *Improving schools from within: Teachers, parents, and principals can make the difference.* San Francisco, CA: Jossey-Bass.

Bitterman, A., Goldring, R., and Gray, L. (2013). Characteristics of public and private elementary and secondary school principals in the United States: Results from the 2011–12 schools and staffing survey (NCES 2013-313). Washington, DC: National Center for Education Statistics.

Black, J. A., and English, F. W. (2001). *What they don't tell you in schools of education about school administration.* Lanham, MD: Scarecrow Press.

Boyer, E. L. (1983). *High school: A report on secondary education in America.* New York, NY: Harper & Row.

Burkhauser, S., Gates, S. M., Hamilton, L. S., and Schuyler Ikemoto, G. (2012). First-year principals in urban school districts: How actions and working conditions relate to outcomes. Santa Monica, CA: RAND Corporation.

Collins, J. C. (2001). *Good to great. Why some companies make the leap . . . and others don't.* New York, NY: HarperBusiness.

Copland, M. A. (2001, March). The myth of the superprincipal. *Phi Delta Kappan, 82*(7), 528–33.

Covey, S. R. (2004). *The 7 habits of highly effective people: Restoring the character ethic.* [Rev. ed.]. New York: Free Press.

Cronin, A. (2016). Student-led conferences: Resources for educators. Retrieved from www.edutopia.org/blog/student-led-conferences-resources-ashley-cronin

Csikszentmihalyi, M. (1990). *Flow: The psychology of optimal experience.* New York, NY: Harper & Row.

Day, C. (2007, Fall). What being a successful principal really means: An international perspective. *Educational Leadership and Administration, 19,* 13–24.

Desravines, J., Aquino, J., and Fenton, B. (2016). *Breakthrough principals: A step-by-step guide to building stronger schools.* San Francisco, CA: Jossey-Bass.

DuFour, R., DuFour, R., Eaker, R., and Many, T. (2006). *Learning by doing: A handbook for professional learning communities at work.* Bloomington, IN: Solution Tree.

Dwyer, D. C. (1984, February). The search for instructional leadership: Routines and subtleties in the principal's role. *Educational Leadership, 41*(5), 32–37.

Frankl, V. (1984). *Man's search for meaning: An introduction to logotherapy.* New York, NY: Touchstone.

Fullan, M. (2010, March/April). The awesome power of the principal. *Principal, 89*(4), 10–15.

Fullan, M. (2014). *The principal: Three keys to maximizing impact*. San Francisco, CA: Jossey-Bass.

Fuller, E. J. (2012, July 17). Examining principal turnover. Retrieved from http://nepc.colorado.edu/blog/examining-principal-turnover

Greenleaf, R. K. (1977). *Servant leadership: A journey into the nature of legitimate power and greatness*. Mahwah, NJ: Paulist Press.

Hart, L. A. (1989). The horse is dead. Phi Delta Kappan, 71(3), 237–242.

Hattie, J. A. C. (2009). *Visible learning: A synthesis of over 800 meta-analyses relating to achievement*. New York, NY: Routledge.

Honeycutt, L. (2011). Aristotle's rhetoric. Retrieved from http://rhetoric.eserver.org/aristotle/

Leithwood, K., Mascall, B., Strauss, T., Sacks, R., Memon, N., and Yashkina, A. (2007). Distributing leadership to make schools smarter: Taking the ego out of the system. *Leadership and Policy in Schools, 6*, 37–67.

Leithwood, K., Seashore Louis, K., Anderson, S., and Wahlstrom, K. (2004). How leadership influences student learning. Retrieved from http://www.walacefoundation.org/knowledge-center/Pages/How-Leadership-Influences-Student-Learning.aspx

National Education Association. (2015). *Rankings and estimates: Rankings of the states 2014 and estimates of school statistics 2015*. Washington, DC: National Education Association.

Pink, D. (2009). *Drive: The surprising truth about what motivates us*. New York, NY: Riverhead Books.

Resourceful Manager. (2016). Leaders vs. managers: 17 traits that set them apart [infographic]. Retrieved from https://www.resourcefulmanager.com/leaders-vs-managers

Safe and Civil Schools. (2016). Program preview for start on time! Retrieved from http://www.safeandcivilschools.com/products/program_previews.php

Schmidt, L. J. (2002). *Gardening in the minefield: A survival guide for school administrators*. Portsmouth, NH: Heinemann.

Sizer, T. R. (1984). Compromises. *Educational Leadership, 41*(6), 34–37.

United States Department of Labor. (2016). U.S. bureau of labor statistics, employment projections program. Retrieved from http://www.bls.gov/ooh/management/elementary-middle-and-high-school-principals.htm#tab-6

Whitaker, T. (2003). *What great principals do differently: Fifteen things that matter most*. Larchmont, NY: Eye on Education, Inc.

About the Author

Robert Cunard grew up in Southern California and attended the University of California, Berkeley, where he earned a degree in rhetoric and was a member of the rowing team. Upon graduation, he returned to Southern California and began a career as a secondary English teacher. During his 15 years as a classroom teacher, Robert taught in urban and suburban settings, coached basketball and tennis, and served as a high school activities director. He earned his master's in educational administration at California State University, Long Beach, and continued his graduate education at Pepperdine University, where he earned a doctorate in education.

Following his 15 years of classroom teaching, Robert became an assistant principal in the Newport-Mesa Unified School District, where he served for nine years in three different high schools. He was appointed principal of La Sierra High School, located in the city of Riverside, where he served for four years. Robert and his team led La Sierra to dramatic improvements in academic achievement, graduation rates, and college attendance rates. He returned to Orange County to serve as principal at Magnolia High School, located in Anaheim just minutes from Disneyland. During his six years as principal, the school improved in academic achievement by all measures. In 2016, Robert was honored by the Association of California School Administrators as the Orange County region's Secondary Principal of the Year. He retired from his administrative career in 2016 to write *The Successful Principal*.

www.ingramcontent.com/pod-product-compliance
Lightning Source LLC
Chambersburg PA
CBHW021851300426
44115CB00005B/115